The Position of Psychographic Variables on Target Markets

Abduljalil Sarli
Rohaizat Baharun

The Position of Psychographic Variables on Target Market

Segmentation and Marketing

LAP LAMBERT Academic Publishing

Impressum/Imprint (nur für Deutschland/only for Germany)
Bibliografische Information der Deutschen Nationalbibliothek: Die Deutsche Nationalbibliothek verzeichnet diese Publikation in der Deutschen Nationalbibliografie; detaillierte bibliografische Daten sind im Internet über http://dnb.d-nb.de abrufbar.
Alle in diesem Buch genannten Marken und Produktnamen unterliegen warenzeichen-, marken- oder patentrechtlichem Schutz bzw. sind Warenzeichen oder eingetragene Warenzeichen der jeweiligen Inhaber. Die Wiedergabe von Marken, Produktnamen, Gebrauchsnamen, Handelsnamen, Warenbezeichnungen u.s.w. in diesem Werk berechtigt auch ohne besondere Kennzeichnung nicht zu der Annahme, dass solche Namen im Sinne der Warenzeichen- und Markenschutzgesetzgebung als frei zu betrachten wären und daher von jedermann benutzt werden dürften.

Coverbild: www.ingimage.com

Verlag: LAP LAMBERT Academic Publishing GmbH & Co. KG
Heinrich-Böcking-Str. 6-8, 66121 Saarbrücken, Deutschland
Telefon +49 681 3720-310, Telefax +49 681 3720-3109
Email: info@lap-publishing.com

Approved by: Malaysia, Universiti Teknologi of Malaysia (UTM)

Herstellung in Deutschland:
Schaltungsdienst Lange o.H.G., Berlin
Books on Demand GmbH, Norderstedt
Reha GmbH, Saarbrücken
Amazon Distribution GmbH, Leipzig
ISBN: 978-3-8473-1742-5

Imprint (only for USA, GB)
Bibliographic information published by the Deutsche Nationalbibliothek: The Deutsche Nationalbibliothek lists this publication in the Deutsche Nationalbibliografie; detailed bibliographic data are available in the Internet at http://dnb.d-nb.de.
Any brand names and product names mentioned in this book are subject to trademark, brand or patent protection and are trademarks or registered trademarks of their respective holders. The use of brand names, product names, common names, trade names, product descriptions etc. even without a particular marking in this works is in no way to be construed to mean that such names may be regarded as unrestricted in respect of trademark and brand protection legislation and could thus be used by anyone.

Cover image: www.ingimage.com

Publisher: LAP LAMBERT Academic Publishing GmbH & Co. KG
Heinrich-Böcking-Str. 6-8, 66121 Saarbrücken, Germany
Phone +49 681 3720-310, Fax +49 681 3720-3109
Email: info@lap-publishing.com

Printed in the U.S.A.
Printed in the U.K. by (see last page)
ISBN: 978-3-8473-1742-5

Copyright © 2011 by the author and LAP LAMBERT Academic Publishing GmbH & Co. KG and licensors
All rights reserved. Saarbrücken 2011

THE POSITION OF PSYCHOGRAPHIC VARIABLES ON TARGET MARKET

ABDULJALIL SARLI

ROHAIZAT BAHARUN

ABDULJALIL SARLI   and   ROHAIZAT BAHARUN

EMAILS:

sabduljalil2@live.utm.my

m-rohaizat@utm.my

PHONE: +60- 147016225

ADDRESS :

Faculty of Management and Human Resource Development

(FPPSM), Universiti Teknologi Malaysia, UTM Skudai

81310, Johor, Malaysia.

CONTENTS

PREFACE

The globalization of markets is concentrated to patronize the customers in the basis of their purchasing behaviors. Since consumer behavior is a broad area in the marketing literature, so the behaviors of consumer can be partitioned in the segments such as pre-purchasing, in-time-purchasing, and post-purchasing. Each part has own circumstances which are related such factors like motivation, budget, price, quality and so on. The psychologically processing from feeling needs to post-purchasing is very complicated process. Absolutely, different people have different situations or circumstances to present themselves as customers. The best approach for distinguishing behavior is related to benchmark of psychographic variables.

The first step of marketing is related to discover relationship between the origin of needs and loyalty. Hence, there is a causal relationship among constructs which are intervening in this process. In addition, the formulated research is as an achievement tool to find out to realize the psychographic variables as well as to conduct right customers towards right products. This is the most powerful strategy of marketing. This strategy will not be stable or generalize to other people e.g. has different cultures or even religions. Because, different situation of lifecycle, personality, economical and social events are influencing in the out coming of results of behaviors.

In fact, the aim of this book is to determine the position of psychographic variables on the target market based on the literature of marketing. Also, we consider three chapters which are general discussion, segmentation and tourism marketing which are involved to psychographic variables:

Chapter 1. This chapter is developed by considering the subjects which are pertaining to general issues of psychographics. However, the subjects approximately clear that how can the psychographic variables are interested; and they are inseparable elements of consumer behaviors from starting process of purchasing.

Chapter 2. The marketers understand better the customers, when they have accurate information or data from the customers. Hence, the segmentation issue is a big opportunity to collect more important information of consumer behavior with perceiving differences and similarities among customers.

Chapter 3. Tourism marketing has become more profitable markets for developing countries. This market needs more to distinguish customers' lifestyles and personalities. Therefore, the psychographic variables are influenced in the strategies of marketing to attracting more tourists. Although psychographic variables are interesting in tourism research, there are different situations to understand consumers yet.

In sum up, the literature of marketing presents different glances of the position psychographic variables in variety markets. As a result, the value from the customers is acted as attitude which is originated by employing means-end chains on the base of psychographic variables. Consequently, the chapters are represented consumer behavior from the psychographic traits from the preliminary researches and almost are to explain the relationships of psychographic constructs.

List of Tables

List of Figures

CHAPTER 1

BACKGROUND OF PSYCHOGRAPHICS

1.1 Introduction

Any time markets and customers expose on changing new technology and strategies which encounter new measures for factors of marketing. Changing is a concept that along with or counter front of pros and cons. Consequently, new measures are creating new abilities which can be adapted new techniques. Further, our lifestyle and personality are not except from these changes. Hence, there are such strategies to present psychographic variables are not only very useful but also helpful to understand customer behavior and consumer patterns.

In fact, mass marketing is formed by many people, markets and their relationships to each other. In this case, the customers follow to their needs and wants, whereas the marketers should want to predict demands as well as fulfill the demands at right time and places. Also, merchandises should be distributed among the right people. Undoubtedly, just only mass producing with good quality isn't working for both investors and consumers nowadays; because the circumstances of people are changed by using new technologies. The customers' attitudes and their cognition are affected by many factors which exert through advertising of mass media and Word- of- Mouth (WOM). Therefore, the marketers or researchers pursue the best way to determine desire of consumers. Since some studying of markets are presented that the people should be segmented based on needs and wants, the key of successful firms understand their customers with their perceptions. The observation of markets witness the number of customers with different prefers, different ideas and different glances which are increasingly formed. Hence, the buyers' thinks have been changed by accessing the knowledge which surrounding themselves as well (Ng, 2005). The critical points testified the investment at the marketing really need to estimation of market by marketing researchers, because without the planning and strategies the holders are encountered more risk for their capital.

In addition, the hospitality sections as more profitable markets are not except from these premises. Also, hospitality industry is swiftly developing by considering as important economical resources for each country. On the other hand, Stakeholders should be precisely considered towards to tourism marketing. Moreover, the travelers are as the tourists have belonged to different classified which emanate from their geographical and psychological characteristics with their finances. Hence, the main reason of segmentation at Tourism Market is diversity of products and services which changing simultaneously new strategies that are related to eco-society of each country (Diaz-Martin et al., 2000).

1.2 Psychographics and Segmentation

The structure of segmentation of markets has been oriented on price theory from economics as well as its effects to attain high profit level from different groups of consumers. Smith (1956) mentioned that changing of consumers caused to adjust maturely products. In addition, suppliers attempted to attain more demands by targeting markets (Kotler, 1997, P.250). Hence, focusing on consumers through firms is the best way to measuring customer satisfaction level. In fact, the aim of segmentation is to attempt towards developing marketing and its capabilities in the markets. McDonald and Dunbar (2004) offered that this approach can tailor and manage allocated budget and products in the useful manner. Consequently, the planning of segments can assist marketers to percept better their customers (Dibb et al., 2002). Although most of the researchers sought essentials variables to proper segments of mass markets in 1950s, this conception initiated in 1960s. Twedt(1964) suggested to marketers that they are focusing on more customers who are giving more profits to them. Because of 80 percent of consumption are becoming from half of customers by certain manner in strategic marketing.

Undoubtedly, segmentation has become as a key strategy in the marketing. Kotler (1997) suggested STP (Segmenting, Targeting, Promoting) model which has basic characteristics for segmenting markets such as measurable, substantial, accessible, stable and actionable before the segment implementation. The influencing factors from segmentation approach depend on the customers and organizations. So the researchers released to customers for predicting models of consumption.

As far as, the Consequences of research segmentation from different societies and cultures lead to grow market segmentations as a global market. In other words, nowadays free businesses completely need to contribute in patronizing of consumers for sustaining their firms (Harcar and Kaynak, 2008). Thereby, markets are divided to submarkets which have more common wants and needs of customers. In fact, segmentation is an important strategy to acquire target market from clustering consumers based on their needs and wants, besides it can provide useful information emanated from W-questions which help marketers to better understand consumers. Moreover, the marketers can cope to achieve a proper plan for their specific products or services by considering segmentation as a efficiency strategy. Markets can be segmented based on variety variables such as geographical, demographics, psychographics, and behavioral variables (Kolter, 1977). Each market can be segmented if it has some circumstances such as measurability, substantial, accessible, stable, actionable and responsiveness (Lin 2002). Each of psychographic segmentation approaches has own circumstances, specific time and places, so may be the results from them are not working in other situations. So, the researcher should do rigorously studying respect to different situations namely demographics, geographical and running time of plans. In addition, marketing message can be addressed and identified easily by segmenting markets (Yeoh, 2005).

Psychographic and lifestyle traits are factors for usage products or services which can gain from environment and society situations rather than standard characteristics of person. In fact, lifestyle is a list of relationship among casual behaviors which are recognized casual traits of behaviors. In addition, life has many stages for individuals; major role of life can be formed in different times such as wedding, finding job, education levels, different situations and other important factors affecting life routes in important stages. Marketers should distinguish variety stages of life and accompany values in lifestyles (Tam andTai, 1998). Although segmentation based on lifestyle can lead to important information which would be helpful for product positioning, perceiving multinational societies, and enhancing on international marketing ; those are not stable and continuously change(Wells, 1975). The variables of psychographics have been estimated the variety of consumer behavior dimensions. Further, there are some researches about psychographic segmentation that use in different circumstances as products and services. They are conducted to several features such as VALS, AIO, etc. Most of them are surveyed around lifestyles, values, and personality relationships (Gonzalez and Bello, 2002).

Lifestyle as a main variable of psychographic was suggested by Howard and Sheth (1969) as culture and its values, later Engel et al. (1978; 1990) was carried out about shopping decisions which was based on lifestyles, personality and evolution of psychographic segmentation. Further, Rivas (1997) offered a model that used psychographics on motivation. Generally, the criteria of markets were adjusted with kinds of setting householders and variety of consumer behaviors, therefore affecting of these broad change would be inevitable on people's lifestyles. However, the best model of segmentation would be responsible to dynamic desires or new demands through the consumers and it should be creating balance between supply and demands. Pearce

(1991) presented a model of tourism which was established on Maslow's hierarchy and tourists' motivations (Gonzalez and Bello, 2002).

Generally, customers use products which affaire to forming their personality and social positions. For example, apparel is affecting at classified customers as people judge others from their appearances. So clothing can influence on consumers at their identity and their social groups which they are belonging them or wish to belong them (Dodd et al., 2000).

The customers always search or pursue shops that are adopting with their self-image. Also, consumers who are openness respect to new products are innovativeness, because of reflecting their personalities. In addition, marketing researchers can use this factor as a personality variable to segment markets with having valuable role for research of companies (Cowart et al., 2008). Further, making a decision of customers is a mental process that is obtained by purchasing and consuming specific products.

Culture influences values for presenting lifestyle patterns which can affect on purchase behavior, and then buyers' behaviors can be evaluated after shopping. For instance, values and interests can be reflected by shopping apparel of individuals. Hence, the marketers can achieve their goal with having good knowledge about definition of culture from consumers' values (Hyllegard et al., 2005). On the other hand, satisfaction level from purchasing products or services leads to values which are repeating more in purchasing products and services. Also there is distinct behaviors accompany with individuals who purchased more than less (Kim, 2005).

1.3 Psychographic and Tourism Marketing

Each of psychogrphic variables which are considered in the market, it can be as a precise variable in tourism marketing (Gonzalez and Bello, 2002). The tourism market is one of the important sections of economical marketplace. It could be allocated around US$ 2billion of daily revenue (Future Brands, 2006), as well as, approximately 12 percent of the people who used the international flight as tourists in the world (IATA, 2007; WTTC, 2007). Absolutely, the good performances and implementations sectors of the destination can affect on improving the tourism sectors as value branding. Macro-environments, geographic constraints, history and culture, political status, target customers, services and feedback of tourism issues are factors which can be reasons why is getting better planning for tourist markets, since they are related to main factors (Balakrishnan, 2009). Also, the best strategy to attracting more tourists may be employing of psyche and personality constructs to understanding of customers; as well as the marketers give them right messages and facilities like discount or promotion for branding destination.

In addition, impression of the tourists is valuable point as much as the perception of services. The residential people convey the culture and the vision towards tourist glances. The national culture with destination brands has consistency role respect to strategy of marketing (Simeon, 2006). The products and services of tourism locations with whole facilities are represented their capabilities and development which can be considered as the tourist impressions. According to Balakrishnan (2008), the special strategies for a tourism place are namely essential base working, utilities of nature, adaption of opinions and creating positive policy. The stakeholders should consider to increasing security, presenting the variety of tourism programs that are making more loyalty customers. The tourism venues are noticed by composing business and recreation aims (Hankinson, 2005, 2004); also such new strategies of marketing exert entertainment locations, shopping centers, eco-tourism and culture in the tourism planning. The likelihood of choosing destinations is being more when the marketers can determine specific segments from target markets. In fact, the segmentation by planning is more effective which is caused to increasing the level of loyalty and efficiency of policy. Hence, The raising investment return states that the destinations is considered as a brand, since the cost of attracting tourists for the governments is US$ 1480 billion in the world (WTTC, 2007). Therefore, the destinations should be started by coordinating residents who are coped to deliver experience of travelling on the tourist visions.

Moreover, tourism industry is developed by forming different sections which need to implement as a unit organization. When the consumers are purchasing some services as intangible goods before experiences them, these firms should perform as multi-culture marketing units. Consequently, cross-culture of different countries is led to ranking values and lifestyles. Because a tourist as an individual has own values and lifestyles without his/her culture (Harcar and Kaynak, 2008).

A traditional model of tourists' behavior identifies that pre-purchase, consumption and post-consumption are presented as three levels of purchasing process for tourism products or services. Generally, the first level can be started with tourist's needs or problems then consumers will follow own responses to select the best solutions. At the second level, the tourist will interact with service providers based on his/her evaluations. In the post-consumption, the tourist has estimated received services from providers respect to his/her expectations. Before the consumption level, the traveler faces some risks that may be confronted with them at the destination. Also, the measure of risk is determined by its credibility of information and sources as following facets:

1- Performance risk is leaded by service or product that cannot fulfill the tourist's needs.

2- Financial risk is due to the service doesn't have value of the costs because it is an expensive price or without quality.

3- Time risk is the trip which is just worse the time.

4- Physical risk is due to from safety aspects, because the destination isn't safe for visitor.

5- Psychological risk is happened through the social and psyche problems of destination or the weakness of service.

6- Cultural risk is as culture shock that tourist's expectations don't adopt with the culture of the destination.

The marketer should reduce these mentioned risks and implement proper strategies. Marketer should help tourists to access accurate information of services or products which directly conduct them to reliable sources. Accuracy and enough information of destination can cause to increase the chance for attracting more tourists, whereas the inadequate information causes to decrease the potential tourists at the market. Also, the primary way to attracting tourist is word-of-mouth (WOM) from relatives or friends. Marketers can use indirectly WOM way by giving consultant for reducing the risks. Moreover, the competitors take advantage through decreasing consultant programs by giving adequate information to the tourists with good strategies such as promotions or incentives. Consequently, they use new products and new markets for attracting more tourists. Therefore, marketers should provide the tourists' needs and desires by developing destination and its facilities, as well as care about their loyalty and unwillingness occurrences that make them unhappiness from unpleasant experiences of different products at different places (Reisinger and Turner, 1999).

The main key point of right strategy is to have correct channel to communicate of customers with tourism firms. Communication of market can influence on purchaser or tourists because of semiotics. Hence, classifying situations and social roles of individuals cause to change consumption prototypes. Customers by considering their socio-cultural roles often appear in their aspirations on requesting services or intangible products (Morrison et al., 1999). Moreover, semiotics can be divided to icon, index and symbol which involve to consumers' psyche at the communication market. Indeed, semiotics is served as tools for warning consumers by ads, mass media and social associates. As a result, specialists interpret the meaning of semiotics on the base of the consumers' emotions and psychological responses .Generally, customers would like to real their aspirations or desires from thinks to actualizing (Douglas and Isherwood, 1979). Therefore, the hospitality establishes have been done services which can lead to actualize their customers' desires or aspirations (Gillespie, 1999).

1.4 Customer Satisfaction

However, the hub of the research in consumer behavior is customer satisfaction which is considered more in the literature of marketing as an affective or emotional variable. The customer satisfaction at the tourism market can be acquired by evaluating of products and services attributes simultaneously (Pizam and Ellis, 1999). The previous researches stated that the attributes of the destination are measured to judge through customers who are using services and products from their satisfaction level. In addition, their attribute are divided to three categories namely the material product, attitude and behavior, and the environment. In measurement of attributes for global market, there are cross-culture differences for the levels of customer satisfaction. Since cultures have important roles in order to evaluate attitudes, solution of problems, and the level of capabilities, so they influence on different level of satisfaction as well.

The relationship between satisfaction and revisit intentions of the destination can be moderated by loyalty as a fundamental component of tourist behavior (Bigne et al., 2001). Hsu et al. (2009) claimed that loyalty level can be predicted by using Structural Equation Modeling (SEM) which considers the model with loyalty construct as a reaction tourist behavior to repurchase of specific product or service. In fact, they attempt to present loyalty as a predicted variable and tourism behavior intention. it is due to communications and relationships from the constructs like customer service, web function, and local characteristics. Indeed, loyal customers have different behaviors, because their attitudes respect to products or services can assists delivering commercial messages and reducing the cost of ads. As a result, subjective norms of loyal customers are completely consistence with their psychological traits; attitudes have played precise role to achieve the loyalty.

1.5 Service Quality

Service quality is influencing on consumers' attitudes as factor which is associated to psychographic constructs. Especially, it is the closest variable to customer satisfaction in the marketing literature. Baker and Crompton (2000) demonstrated that there is a really relationship between service quality and customer satisfaction. However, it can state that evaluating performance service quality is approximately similar of evaluating customer satisfaction level from the expectation levels. Also, they confirmed that there are many latent variables among their relationships as extraneous. Hence, satisfaction has become an opportunity which can be represented as the customer experiences; the consequence of this behavior can be presented as affective system by showing emotions or feelings through consumed service or product. Therefore, satisfaction is affected by social-psychological variables which cannot be monitored by service providers.

According the study of Baker and Crompton (2000), Service quality as a construct is a set of relevant performances which are perceived by tourist experiences at the specific destination as a service product. Also, their study has pointed that there is a weak correlation between tourist satisfaction and service quality. Because the extraneous variables are intervening as the mediating effect constructs between quality and satisfaction. Thereby, these mediating effects are the consequence of psychological variables. However, tourism sector is considered an integrated set as a service of the destinations and amalgam stakeholders. Each of these parts is involved to other which has own features and attributes. Hence, service products have active or passive exchanges. In addition, tourists can find out specific service quality by exposing especial promotion or word-of-mouth from acquaintances. Baker and Crompton (2000) confirmed that service quality is counted as attributes of the destination, while satisfaction is a moral concept. In sum up, satisfaction is an experience from cognitive and affective system by interacting the attributes or performances of the specific destination. More differentiates of service quality and satisfaction levels are mentioned in the marketing discussions in 1990s.

1.6 Destination Image

Lee (2009) studied about SEM modeling as path analysis that is about destination image, satisfaction, and behavior intention. The findings of Lee (2009) confirmed that the tourist intentions can be affected by performing the destination and its services. Also, Bigne Alcaniz et al. (2009) illustrated that destination image as cognitive image and future behavior as intentions have associated directly or indirectly. Destination image is a continuum construct which has three parts namely functional, mixed and psychological images. At the first point, Functional facet is related to scenery, accommodation, and price. In addition, psychological aspect is pertaining to atmosphere and friendliness. Therefore, Functional image is involved to the tangible attributes of the specific destination, while psychological image is considered as intangible attribute of the destination. In fact, destination image is a perception from the destination by using means-end chains at the tourists' minds by evoking their ideas, beliefs, feelings and attitudes. Further, tourists face destination image as a pre-purchasing action and then experience services, after traveling or during on-site they would process their experiences which is called behavior intentions as a post-purchasing action.

1.7 Cognitive and Affective Systems

According to study of Byon and Zhang (2010), more researchers of hospitality industry explored to find relationships between subjective issues (affective) and objective issues (cognitive). Most of them are concerned in the main issues of causal structure and distribution channel as tourism investigations. Also, they considered about scale of revisit intention and recommend intention of the destination. Also, estimating destination image is related to positive perceptions which have been encountered with variety scales from the attributes of the destination. Byon and Zhang (2010) have surveyed on sport event as tourism product.

Generally, destination image are divided to three groups of images like organic, induced and complex images (Byon and Zhang, 2010). Organic image is called to find information from geographical publishes, reports of TV, and newspaper or magazine articles, induced image is called to find information from brochures or the internet of specific website destination as well. The main difference between them is related to motivation or intention for travelling, because an individual may be have organic image without motivation of travelling but the individual with induced image often researches accurate information or promotion of the destination. Also, cognitive and affective issues are considered as functional, psychological factors and mixed

13

factors. The functional image is called to tangible (cognitive) of service like scenery, facilities, accommodation as well as psychological image is called to intangibles (affective) factors such as culture, emotional atmosphere. The destination image is related directly or indirectly to people's social and psychological aspects. Moreover, functional image is associated to revisit intention and psychological image is associated to recommend of the destination.

1.8 The Importance of Psychographic variables

Psychographic variables can communicate relationships of consumers' values and products' values. Influencing in consumers' psychographics traits will be very useful for marketers who understood the proper needs and wants through their consumers. Consequently, they can tailor properly their strategies towards target markets by using properly approaches of segmentation. Segmentation is a powerful technique and a tool which can be categories specific people in order to establish subgroups as target markets with different capabilities. At the marketing, recognizing relationships of psychographic variables with product values and their position is creating a precise point, because these strategies are caused to come out the best information from adapted behavior of consumers.

In 1990s, more researchers have propounded the relationships between service quality and satisfaction that are related to latent variables (Baker and Crompton, 2000). Also, marketing aspect has pointed out that there are such intervening psychological constructs between quality and satisfaction, because satisfaction is a judgment thorough service performance as quality which the consumer can experience it as well as fulfilled consumer's quest (Oliver, 1997, P40, P184). In addition, satisfaction is just measuring in order to assessing service quality which has undertaken (Taylor and Baker, 1994, P 166). In other hand, Baker and Crompton (2000) found that there are many psychological variables which are acting as intervening variables between implementation of service and tourists' satisfaction levels. In fact, service providers experienced tourists' behaviors as responses towards their performances and service quality. Antecedent researches have introduced different dimensions beyond of service which are involved with social-psychological constructs. Moreover, service providers could not control these extraneous events (Baker and Crompton, 2000).

Consequently, the applied model of psychographics could be determined that how the target markets should be chosen. Hence, the marketers would be able to distinguish that what amenities and facilities done appropriate with needs and wants of the tourists as well. Although the psychographics model can be reliable model to grasp the attraction of the customers' desire, the results have been different effective or efficiency in different communities. Furthermore, the changing circumstances from socially, economically, politically, technologically and environmentally cause to differentiate results in psychographic segmentation. Hence new modeling of psychographic segmentation can be made easy some implementation or understanding better situation in the future for improving goods and services as the following reasons :

1- New causal relationships are based on psychographics segmentation which it can update consumption patterns.
2- Efficacy techniques of marketing strategies are directly or indirectly involved to psychographic segmentations.
3- Analysis of psychological findings from psychographic constructs influence on consumer behaviors.

1.9 Conclusion

In sum up, marketers always follow to understand customers and promote proper products in the basis of patronizing purchasers. Changing tech and creating new features cause to change consumer needs and wants. In addition, the markets and providers are challenging to attract customers by adapting these changes; and response to the tourists' desires. However, those are employing psychographic segmentation as a feature which can be given them enough information by mixing marketing and stakeholders attempts to find fascinated way to attract consumers. There are different aspects in impact of tourism marketing, as well as the hospitality markets are developed towards globalization by using segmentation to provide amalgam facilities with service quality and other circumstances. Hence, the destination image is influenced by psychographic constructs. Nevertheless, high fulfillments of psychographic variables lead to loyalty of customers or behavior intentions to repurchase of products or services; there are many exploratory topics on the psychographic studying. Hence, the next chapter is explained more rigorously about psychographic details.

CHAPTER 2

Psychographic Segmentation

2.1 Consumer Behavior

The literature of consumer behavior is being broadly issue as academic research, so this section would be conducted to previous researches of psychographic segmentation and its relevant issues towards sustain loyalty discussions at the segmentation. Moreover, their relationships surveys from the marketing literature across their variables. Generally, segmentation is a precise strategically manner that marketers directly or indirectly implement it to understand better consumers through their needs and wants. Antecedents of segmentation and its factors are stated the importance of customer behavior dimensions. Hence, the aim of investigating market evidences is to find evolution modern marketing about consumer behavior and psychographic segmentation at the marketing research. Many of researchers focused on this area to explore specific knowledge from consumers and markets.

2.2 Segmentations and Performances in Marketing

Marketing is developed by forming in the base of rules and disciplines. Also, they are regulated through the past thoughts and new methods by the marketing intelligences. Hence, the historical research of marketing is evoked to establish marketing from economical science, political studying, human resources knowledge, and statistical science. Moreover, it is developed as academic science which refers to the early twentieth century through liberty of scholars about consumer behavior, markets, products and services. Fisher's theory "F-test" by Fisher in 1925 and segmentation theory by Smith in 1956 are evidences of the first using segmentation concept as an empirical research at the real market (Jones and Keep, 2009). In addition, Beane and Ennis in1987 have considered segmentation broadly at the marketing literature (olsen et al., 2009). Moreover, Segmenting market is implemented based on a set of variables which fulfill similar needs and wants for homogenous subgroups.

Wedel and Kamakura are known as pioneers to introduce variables of segmentation in 1998. According to Kahle and Chiagouris(1996), the researches of a few decades testify the evolution of these variables, there isn't clear borderline between two variables of segmentation. Hence, the market can be segmented by Geographical, Demographic, Psychographic and Behavioral variables (Kolter, 1977). Segmentation is strategies for a mass market that converts to submarkets, while they have own segments with special characters. According to Lin (2002), McCarthy in 1981, Pride and Ferrell in 1983 have pointed out the experiences of segmentation based on consumers' desires. Also, Kotler (1997) proposed that there are three stages for achieving to right segmentation by using STP (Segmenting, Targeting, and Positioning) technique. At first, marketers have to divide customers to subgroups on the base of specific variables which can be distinguished similarities in the consumers' needs and wants respect to specific products. Next, they should evaluate each segments by considering more profitable customers for the firms, this level is known as targeting. So, the marketers can select one or more segments by concerning their competitors and doing the best. Finally, marketers should achieve to good position for their products in order to help customers by identifying advantages through positioning, selecting correct advantages, and inspired good positioning to customers (Bown, 1998).

Table 2.1 : History of Segmentation and its Evolution

Decades	Historical Segmentation	Developments
2000s	predicting segmentation models(Kardon,1990; Van Raaij, 1993; Brown, 1995; Firat and Katesh, 1997; Firat and Shultz, 1997; Sheth et al., 2000)	The manners were not good tailored customers.
1990s	Performance had problems (Littler, 1992; Piercy and Morgan, 1993; Dibb and Simkin, 1997)	Determined the problems of performance and surveyed validity of questions
1980s	VALs and VALS2(Mitchell, 1983) coming up psychographic variables(Burns and Harrison , 1979; Lastovicka, 1982)	Advanced psychographic segmentation
1970s	Stability of segmentation(Green and wind, 1973; Bishop et al.,1975; Blattberg and Sen, 1976; Burgher and Schott, 1972)	Origin to use of new models for segmenting
1960s	Initiating segmentation(Webster, 1965; Pessemier et al., 1967; Bass et al., 1987)	Initiating for selecting lifestyle variables
1950s	Starting point of segmentation from industrial market concentration	Geographic and categories of products

Source: Quinn et al (2007)

Raaij and Verhallen (1994) stated that there is a strategy as segmentation on the base of products or services situations. They have recognized three different situations for traits of products or services namely general, domain-specific and specific level of consuming products or services. General level is considered as the most establish attribute situation respect to other two groups. Moreover, they have stated such behaviors as three divisions as single acts, domain-behavior and behavioral patterns. Single act refers to the action which can be easily observed from body language, but domain-behavior should be inferred from groups of single acts. Also, behavioral patterns can be formed by set of behavioral groups that acts together as unique like lifestyles. Therefore, domain-behavior is the consequence of acting several behaviors in common ways. Hence, they can influence in behavioral patterns.

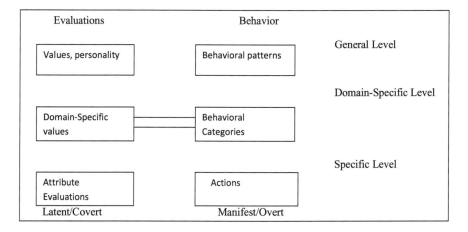

Figure 2.1 Customers Features as Demand Size

Source: Raaij and Verhallen(1994)

A perfect segmentation is becoming a powerful strategy that can be conducted both consumers and marketers to attain extremely profits. Segmentation of products or services is adjusting based on tailored method of consumer desires. In addition, changing market policy is due to appear differentiating in time and place. Hence, Segmentation is obtained from differentiate among the relations of the consumer values and consumption patterns. Therefore, consumers use means-end chain systems to achieve their consequences from evaluating values.

Raaij and Verhallen (1994) proposed that there are such attributes of proper segmentation as the following:

1- Typifying the segments(Identification, Measurability)
2- Homogeneity(Variation, Stability, Congruity)
3- Usefulness (Accessibility, Sustainability)
4- Strategic Criteria (Potentiality, Attractiveness).

Ng (2005) proposed that there are simple ways to attain customers' information at the olden days respect to nowadays, because the behavior of customers and the consumption patterns are changed. The new methods of selling are improved towards globalization for seeking out the customers in the world. The tactics are retaining customers based on loyalty program with increasing product choices and refining offer packages to the customers on the right time. Also, the customers conduct to right firm with legal tender to be segmented at the direct market. In addition, the consumer's self-selection is due to choice products or services by themselves. Hence, the customers create value, and then the firm can distinguish segments by acquiring the information from self-selection products of customers. Further, training staff should be warned not to avoid value of products, because they can cause to reduce the cost of selling and promotion. Moreover, segmentation at the direct market with self-selection can be based on the following formulations:

1- At the market, the kind of product is completely determined for the customer.
2- Each segments gives own products, it means that two different segments should be shown two different products.
3- The customer can have right for selecting the products in own segment.

Once a customer thinks about new product with high value, the marketers provide circumstances for the customer that can be conducted to the right company with good incentives.

2.3 Psychographic Roles

Beatty, Homer and Kahle (1988) accomplished segmenting by mirror approach, and using VALS and LOV process to show measuring psychographic variables with ranking the values and identifying most important values. Beside, products or services are substantial in the markets. They can give value or prestige to the consumers as appropriate social status, as well as are adopted with the lifestyles of customers. In addition, they can divide them along with their socio-status (Lin 2002).In 1994, Raaij and Verhallen segmented market substantially three approaches which are namely forward , backward and simultaneous of relationships between consumer traits and situation of consumption patterns. Henderson and his colleague used empirical segmentation based on brand preferences in 1998.   Whereas Gralopois measured brand preference by loyalty and analyzed it by Logit regression for clustering with estimating consumer satisfaction levels. Early 1990s, segmentation approaches were developed and formed as new ways like VALS, LOV, RVS (Rokeach Values Survey), APT (Association Pattern Technique), and mean-ends chain technique. In addition, Lin (2002) approved that combining several variables of segmentation such as demographics and psychographics simultaneously applying can create precise information of sub-markets.

Some of the researchers believed that the concept of segmentation is obtained from social and economical traits. Haley (1968) witnessed that all of customers are not following same benefits through products or services, so he suggested that it is better to offer variety brands to customers. This model is known as Haley's benefit-based segmentation. Some researcher maintained lifestyle variables which is used for segmentation, the efforts of researchers have led to psychographic segmentations in 1980s especially SRI's International project is known as VALs (Values and Lifestyles) and advanced that (VALs 2). Then, the researchers followed to measure validity and reliability of Psychographic by mixing models in 1990s.

Nowadays, segmentation by psychographic variable is more consider for scholar and marketing to achieve a proper model of segmenting on the markets. Although there is not any clear definition of psychographic variables, they are playing important roles in segmentation methodology on the markets for determining clusters of consumers. Demographic and geographic variables complement the criteria in terms of psychographic segmentation (Beatty et al., 1988). The most researches of behaviors and attitudes have been done psychographic segmentation as popular strategy in 1990s (Harcar and Kaynak, 2008). The psychographic segmentation literature confirmed that each country has own psychographic and demographic variables because of variety ethnics and cultures. However, the starting point of surveying psychographic clustering is leading to lifestyles and personality variables. Consequently, lifestyles variables are involved with activities, interests and opinions (AIO) and personality is included internal and external traits.

One of the best approaches for the better understanding customers is psychographic segmentations. Although the psychological traits determine lifestyles, personalities, values bounded dimensions; they are creating properly information consonant with Demographic characters (Ahmad et al., 2010). Even, the researchers of marketing didn't attain at the coincidence of psychographics definition, there is the greatest issues in the research marketing. In fact, psychographic segmentation is dividing mass market to specific submarkets that marketers can distinguish better own customers. In other words, psychographic segmentation is one of approaches to help marketers for two reasons. At first, it reveals homogenous submarkets. Next, it helps them to opting appropriate methods within target markets. The customers are portioned to groups at the psychographic (Kotler, 1997). Although, the consumers have different psychological needs and wants, the stakeholders and the investors are following the opportunities from lifestyle or personality of consumers who are offered by goods and services properly.

The difference of consumer behaviors cannot be described just with demographic variables and socio-economic factors. Also, improving marketing mix is yielded by using a standard and appropriate strategy as segmentation approaches. Psychographic variables can be measured by employing lifestyle variable on the base of VALs (Values, Attitude, and Lifestyle) and AIO (Activities, Interests, Opinions). Differentiate of purchasing patterns, consumers' sentiments is forecasted with psychographic segmentation, and then the marketers can improve and innovate their goods and services (Gunter and Furham, 1992; Wolburg and Pokrywczynski, 2001).

According to Mitchel (1995), Psychographic is very valuable for marketers and it can facilitate to find the answers the essential problems such as which attributes of products are properly adapting towards the consumers' lifestyles? And which messages of commercial can attract more consumers? In addition,   Psychographic is considered as measuring and analyzing some aspects of consumers such as feelings, thoughts, reflecting, lifestyles, personality and demographic. On the other words, it can be produced tools to the researchers in order to measure quantities of psychological dimensions of customers' situations or segments target market within common traits of consumer behaviors. Psychographic is related to internal traits of person or his/her lifestyle. Sometimes it is focused on specific area of consumer behavior and sometimes on general issues. The variables of psychographic are chosen from standard criteria of lifestyles or personalities, and may be handmade.

According to Beatty et al. (1988) stated that psychographic criteria such as VALS, LOV, and values are difficultly measured. Each approach has own advantages and disadvantages to analyze clustering result from the segmentation, but they can give precise information of consumer behavior.

Raaij and Verhallen (1994) demonstrated three approaches of segmentation that they were applied by similarities on responding consumers to specific-situation of products or services. Those segmentations were forward, backward and simultaneous. Forward segmentation was started with relating to similarities of consumption products or services, backward segmentation was started by considering of similarities of consumers' traits, and simultaneous was based on relationships between consumers' traits and situation-specific consumption patterns. It was distinguished that two categories of consumers' traits which they were general and specific. The general characteristics were demographic, lifestyle and personality, whereas specific formed with their attitudes, opinions, perceptions and preferences. Those characters were determined by analyzing consumer's responses towards consumption of goods or services. However, antecedents of segmentation research stated the approaches used relationships between values and behavioral response of consumers with their traits at the domain-specific level. In this way canonical correlation analysis was very useful to segment.

Orth (2004) have surveyed that the existing differences between perceived criteria and benefit sought for segmentation which use lifestyle emanate from benefit dimensions as value such as quality, price, social and emotional benefits. Also, they have proved the support decisions and brand selecting which have opposed with preferences, lifestyle segments, demographic and behavioral variables. Marketers consider the consumption value of products from consumers as communication product and consumers. In fact, product or service is considered as functional benefits, whereas brand is considered as consumer perceived positive and negative emotional benefit.

Psychographics segmentations can identify almost the expending levels of time and money. In other words, AIO levels of consumers lead to useful information of lifestyles through each of purchasers that how to do in their life, when and where spend the money and time. Tam and Tai (1998) claimed that psychographic segmentation of Chinese Female markets in two phases which examine psychographic statements and improving typology of customers. Also, the authors presented that psychographics variables are pertaining to time and circumstances of socio-economic situation and changeable. In addition, the researcher should be applying rigorously existent similarities and differences among consumers.

Raaij and verhallen (1994) posited that clustering of consumers for segmentation is led to three groups namely general segmentation from psychographic and behavioral variables, product –specific through classifying utility of goods or services, and brand-specific . Further, each of psychographic factors is measuring in one dimension of scale(Tam and Tai 1998).

Moreover, Boedeker (1995) stated that shoppers are formed two clusters as modern buyers and non-modern buyers based on satisfaction. In addition, the clusters have similarities in socio-demographic features, while they have differences in psychographics features. Modern buyers versus non-modern buyers are précised in time, efficiency and convenience of shopping. The clustering method is accomplished on lifestyles such as spending time, money, and mood of shopping. It measures in four factors such as service qualities, place for experience and recreation, efficiency of buying and consciousness of products.

2.3.1 Lifestyle

In fact, lifestyle is as a psychographic variable which can be presented by individual's activations, way of his/her thinks, kind of lives and lifecycle, and his/her performances versus of environment stimulates. In generally, lifestyles can be demonstrated characteristics of consumers and tendency of purchasing behaviors which are related to their experiences from shopping (Harcar and Kaynak, 2008).

Also, Lifestyle is comprised by activities like spending money and time, interests as things which are less or more important degree in customer life, and opinions as the view of customers respect to the environment and his/her world. In fact, lifestyle variable is holistic knowledge that can allow combining consumer's behaviors as his/her characteristics (Gonzales and Bello, 2002).

However, cross-national and cross-cultural are other components of lifestyles to establish lifestyle and personality of consumers (Beatty et al., 1988). Hence, the lifestyle models have been developed for segmentation. For example, VALs system is formed and developed from Maslow hierarchical needs. Also, LOV is established measures that are estimated nine factors of values for psychographic segmentation by the researchers from Michigan University in 1980s. Moreover, It is more accurate approach than VALs as well as providing proper information from clustering(Beatty et al. , 1988).

Hsu and Chang (2008) posited that the effects of related communications between family members and lifestyle of the youth are intervening on shopping behaviors. Also, they consider two items of goods like sport shoes and clothes which have interested as goods or common shopping among university students. In this research, the variables are focused on ten factors of lifestyle that are related to AIO, and then are conducted to clustering students in two clusters. The subgroups have different ways to measure levels of making decision for buying individually of goods. Furthermore, different lifestyles and personalities can conduct the youth to be in several classifies by relevant communication models. Moreover, they use non-hierarchical cluster analysis for clustering and using factor analysis to reduce variables for getting accurate results.

Another aspect of lifestyle is presented by Hur et al. (2010), their research is posited us the segmented market by using lifestyle is showing facts of studying through consumers' feelings and attitudes to the specific products. In other words, it is determining more details from situation of consumption patterns and satisfaction level of consumers. Hence, the survey of relationship between lifestyles and specific products with high tech in order to segment a market is very precise nowadays. Appliance markets and consumption situations are considered as important issues from householders. Also, for measuring the householders attitudes use AIO measuring with consumer's dietary life. Further, standard segmentation by lifestyle can be facilitated decision making or implemented by proper strategy at the market, as well as it can be described as behaviors which cannot explain by other variables. The analysis of lifestyle segmentation can estimate social changes. Moreover, by distinguishing behaviors, feelings and purchasing behaviors the marketing researchers can predict the future of the markets.

2.3.1.1 Attitudes

Indeed, Attitude is a concept in which can process information in mind then make a decision through the buyer. It is involved with beliefs and making decisions as negative or positive view that is evaluated on specific goods or services by relevance ranking such as like-dislike, satisfying-unsatisfying, favor-disfavor, or good-bad. Also, social cognition or learning theory states that attitude is a set of relationships between a person and his/her environment interactions. Moreover, motivation and cognitive abilities are important piles of Bandura's social cognitive theory that argues about self-efficacy system. Further, self –efficacy system is giving ability to a person who can process in own information and action, and then can be showing behavior at his/her environment. It is as a mediator between the cognition and behavior (Yeoh, 2005).

When people have used own attitudes, beliefs and preferences towards products or services, they find out positive or negative feeling respect to the purchasing of goods or services. The related contradiction aspects are known as "Ambivalence". The satisfaction of consumers from their attitudes can be created by psychological factors that are involved by evoking feeling, observation and hearing. In other words, fulfillment of customer expectations through using the products or services is known as "satisfaction" of customer (WTO, 1985). Indeed, making decision as an attitude is more likelihood from customer with satisfaction. But dissatisfaction is a preventive factor for repeat purchasing in the brand marketing literature. Therefore, preferences, beliefs and opinions are influencing in making decision as portions of attitude of customers.

Actually, the most of theories are discussed about attitudes. Often, they consider the people who have positive progress and the people who take advantage from more effective things towards achieve their goals. Hence, some theories describe these aspects with social identities like approval of society and presenting identity (Shavitt,1989). Furthermore, attitudes can be considered as precise role in consumer behavior by implementing of important functions for the customers (Schiffman and Kanuk, 2000, P. 212-213).

2.3.1.2 VALs System

One of main psychographic segmentations is VALs system. In fact, it is developed by values and lifestyles approaches which are established by SRI international firm at the U.S.A in 1980s. Also, this system has popular model which is suggested by Mitchel(1983). On the other hand, it can be clustered by eight clusters of American based on demographic and psychographic variables which is led to VALs (Values and Lifestyles) system. In addition, Japanese VALs model is offered as exploration, self-expression, achievement , adapters, tradition, and realist orientation (Lin, 2002).

Actually, VALs systems are different from country to another country. For example, one research which is carried out as VALs system at Hong Kong in 1990s depicts clustered females based on their attitudes and beliefs in five clusters such as traditionalists, strivers, achievers, and adapters. While, the other cluster analysis is occurred in Taiwan with eight clusters namely traditionalist homebodies, confident traditionalists, discontented moderns, rebellious youths, young strivers , middle-class, family-centered, and lethargic(Tam and Tai, 1998).

VALs, in general, implicates on analyzing psychological purchasers which are in special situations as consumers. In other words, it is shown as existence of correlation between personality characteristics and performances of consumers. Also, VALs considers as psychological evaluations of selected purchasing behaviors which are recognizing motivations and behavioral materialist from behavioral variables as psychographic segmentation (Harcar and Kaynak, 2008).

Also, VALs2 is known as psychographic setting both demographics variables and buyer's consumption styles along with their attitudes. Moreover, SRI institute had published VALs 1 based on Arnold Mitchell's theory which is extended to evolution values of Maslow's hierarchy needs, while VALs 2 is based on using products, and Japan VALs is based on customers' influenced changing values and social behavior criteria (Winters, 1992).

2.3.1.3 AIO

AIO is a feature which can estimate consumers based on effectiveness and cognition systems. This approach is functioning with consumers' activities, Interests, and Opinions. Those can be evaluated different facets of consumers' traits that are related to specific products or services. On the other hand, activities are considered as spending time and money, whereas Interests are engaged with ranking importance objects through consumers. Also, Opinions can be interpreted as knowledge or information of consumers is due to their response from stimulus of environment and the World. In addition, they can be surveyed as general or specific forms. In fact, those measures are estimated the relationships among consumer behaviors and their lifestyles by employing such criteria. Hence, the AIO approach has been carried out among variety conditions of consumers and products as evaluated motivations, preferences and consumers' attitudes towards their activities, interests and opinions (Gonzalez and Bello, 2002).

According to Ahmad et al. (2010), the lifestyle as a construct or factor is an important portion of psychographics segmentation which is oriented by activities, interests and opinions (AIO) of consumers. In fact, AIO approach can produce essential patterns of consumer behaviors, such they can be evaluated through the effect of macro/micro circumstances in the customers' life, as well as explain their attitudes or behaviors based on especial product group or activities (Hawkins et al., 2001). Therefore, lifestyles are settled by AIO factors (Vyncke, 2002).

Another aspect of lifestyle especially in AIO approach is presented from the marketing researchers; the AIO feature can be identified the border or difference through the upscale user and non-user of specific products based on their lifestyles. The researchers interested in to know that the customers what have done in the leisure time or how can be ranking their hobbies, believes, and events which are occurred in their surrounding environment. As well as, the purchasers are what shown in the demographic characteristics when interacts with their lifestyles. Most of working of AIO approach is rating statements which are extended by Wells and Tigert(1971) ,actually a questionnaire is designed with 300 items relevant AIO measuring that are pointed out common works in a day with four dimensions (Lee, 2005).

Table 2.2: Lifestyle Dimensions

Activities	Interests	Opinion	Demographics
Work	Family	Themselves	Age
Hobbies	Home	Social issues	Education
Social events	Job	Business	Income
Vacation	Community	Economics	Occupation
Entertainment	Recreation	Education	Family Size
Club membership	Fashion	Products	Dwelling
Community	Media	Future	Geography
Shopping	Achievements	Culture	City size
Sports			Stage in life cycle

Source : Adopted from Plummer(1974)

According to the study of Ahmad et al. (2010), there are such researches as AIO feature such as profile male innovators , the relationship between time-oriented and lifestyle patterns , the behaviors of women at the food purchasing , general pattern of consuming , to survey psychographic and lifestyle antecedents from expecting of quality services, exploring relationship between behavioral traveling and healthy living (Hallab,1999), verifying the affecting of technology at the new media, surveying of affecting lifestyle dimensions and ethnocentrism on purchasing decision (Kucuckemiroglu et al., 2006); studying of behaviors from tourists' consumption (Gonzalez and Bello, 2002); to identify the lifestyle factors that adopt with affecting the consumers who use the tech products (Lee , 2009); the investigating of cross-cultural study of lifestyle traits from Taiwanese versus U.S. consumers and measuring lifestyles from using AIOs (Tao, 2006).

Harcar and Kaynak (2008) surveyed similarities and differences between two distinct countries by considering psychographic segmentation which is used values and lifestyles variables based on cross-cultures. Also, their finding shows that some values or demographic variables may be similar, but lifestyles are different. Because social and culture components are affected on AIO system which are formed from their affect and cognition system as the lifestyles of consumers.

2.3.1.3.1 Activities

Activities are gained from the acts of the customers' lifestyles in a specific time such as the necessary actions and recreations in a day or works at home. Also, activities can be known as setting of the budgets and times of customers (Ahmad et al., 2010). According to Michman et al.(2003), activities can be led from some actions from activities like sports, occupation, recreation and hobbies. Whole of entertainments, home working, daily working or essential working day-to-day are considered as activities.

2.3.1.3.2 Interests

Ahmad et al. (2010) proposed that interests are considered as ordinal scale measuring among the society, family and home. Furthermore, most of shoppers' behaviors are depending on their psyche that time, also they reveal their behaviors as the level of exciting vs. predictable or unpredictable purchasing. In fact, interests are considered as the customer likes own home, work, family, fashion and food (Michman et al., 2003).

2.3.1.3.3 Opinions

While the customers evaluate their beliefs vs. importance of products or services, at the real time, in fact, they propose their opinions about products or services (Ahmad et al., 2010). Actually social subjects, political issues, education situation, business and forecasting about the future can be considered as opinions of the customers (Michman et al., 2003). One of the most important traits of a person is his/her opinions which help us to measure the indicators for predicting consumer behaviors.

2.3.2 Values

According to study of Roy and Goswami (2007), psychographic variables are latent variables as well as intervening variables which can act as a bridge gap within values and consumer behaviors. In addition, both of values and lifestyle are the consequence of learning from the culture and social norms by personalizing consumers to reveal their personal characteristics. Further, the research of values and lifestyles are more applied than mere demographic variables or socio-economic researches in marketing literature. Also, the type of such researches is more about macro levels than micro levels. In addition, Rokeach (1973, 1979) extended lifestyle segmentation by employing the different dimensions as terminal and instrumental values. Hence, culture is as an effective element on social norms, values, lifestyles of the consumers' tendencies on their purchasing behaviors. As a result, behaviors of shopping are considered as quickly seeking, innovativeness, consciousness-fashion, comparing shoppers, information seeking, brand loyalty, and consumers' habiting (Harcar and Kaynak, 2008).

It is noticeable that the most important feature for attracting consumers is patronizing consumers by considering their values in the environment of products. Absolutely, values are central concept of life that can influence on affective and cognition system. Nowadays, mass media triggers special value on the base of psychographic variables because of efficacy the segmentation. Consequently, the global marketing cause to change psychographic variables and values across the World (Beatty et al., 1988).

In general, values are considered as psychographic variables which can be measured by justifying of consumer behaviors respect to consumption patterns, tendency purchasing or responses of environmental stimulates. Priority and posteriori of values are compared across cultures and societies, because values are stated as individuals' trait patterns which are different among the people who have different societies, because of inherent own values (Harcar and Kaynak, 2008).

The other aspect of values stated that estimating comprehensively from a product or a service can be known as value of product or service. It is an important component of purchasing for consumers because of purchasing and satisfying simultaneously that means the things are received and given by the consumers. In fact, the perceptions of trading-off goods or services represent values of products/services that are sacrificed by customer as paying the price. Also, the most useful elements from benchmarking of consumer's values are quality and price of goods or services. However, values are considered as maintaining or supporting feelings which are important in our life. Consequently, values can be taken as an important variable to measure of satisfaction of consumers as well as better perception as forecasting consumer behavior at the market places for the marketers (Divine and Lepisto, 2005).

In addition, shopping values are directly or indirectly related to the traits of consumers which are psychologically stated as evaluating through using products or services (Michon et al., 2005). So the experiences of shopping and shopping environments can be influenced on purchasing behaviors (Stoel et al., 2004). Hence, the interaction of consumers and products/services is depending on the experience of consumption patterns (Michon et al., 2008). This issue could be shown through the internal or external values of products/services. Therefore, purchasing almost acts as giving benefit to gratify consumers. In that case, purchasing values can be represented as utility and hedonic aspects through customers when they have frequency experiences of shopping (Babin and Attaway, 2000). On the other hand, customers who are perceived more values of excitements of purchasing and aware from fashion-conscious are especially given motivations for purchasing products/services from the social values.

2.3.2.1 LOV

The researchers of Michigan University inspired from Maslow and Feather's system, and produced a list of Values (LOV) as measuring behaviors. It is considered LOV with nine factors which are transformed two sections as internal and external values (Lin 2002). Also, values are considered as factors which are affected on attitudes towards purchase behaviors. In addition, fashion-consciousness and innovativeness as psychographic variables can create positive associate between external values and purchasing behavior (Roy and Goswami, 2007). The study of Roy and Goswami (2007) mentioned that the results come out from apparel products and the relationships of the variables will be different on other products/services which have different values. Further, LOV is known as for oriented from internal and external values of behaviors, so managers focus on this aspect of traits for predicting consumer behaviors (Kropp et al., 2005). Moreover, LOV is due to from Maslow's hierarchy needs by considering nine criteria which are introduced by Kahle (1983) as the following criteria:

1- Fun and enjoyment
2- Security
3- Warm relations with others
4- Sense of accomplishment
5- Self-fulfillment
6- Being well respected
7- Sense of belonging
8- Self-respect
9- Excitement.

2.3.3 Personality

Personality factors as variables are more essential for segmentation than demographic factors. According Lin (2002), one of the best ways to evaluate personality values is Rokeach

Values Survey (RVS). Also, personality values are due to behaviors and perceiving situations of specific product or service. In addition, the results of studying behaviors on special product/service are different from other products/services. Hence, personal values are presented by behaviors or attitudes which are studying through a category of products as well as specific situations (Brunsø et al., 2004).

In addition, social identity of individual is as a real imagine or a reference of a customer which is a part of the context from who is he/she or how he/she would like to be (Reed, 2002, P. 255). Besides, Villani and Wind (1975) stated that Locus of Control (LOC) has been introduced as two type personalities of people. First type of personality involves believing the people can control their life by themselves (Internal Orientation), while the second type is due to the external factors (External Orientation) which can affect their life.

Moreover, recognizing of factors from self-concept patterns pertains to its confirmation about interpersonal and external aspects of social situations. in this case, while one likes to have ideas from others' view or their experiences in order to achieve own goals that it is called external aspect of self-concept. Whereas interpersonal aspect less impact with others' beliefs and he/she accomplishes in own ways. In fact, products and its consumption patterns affect in both external and interpersonal of self-aspects .So, products are very important traits which one possesses to form and support his/her identity. Almost the customers are openness for things which help them to develop their social identity and present their personality which how can appear at their society .The study of Grewal et al. (2000, P.235) stated that products have functions which are related to create social identity of a person as the following tasks:

1- Establishing communication among relationships of a person and others,
2- Gradually fitting a social position to a person who uses the products,
3- Helping to determine a central achievement for a person.

Study of Goldsmith (2002) posited that when the customers are buying more apparel at the market, in fact they attempt to achieve their desires via positive effects of products. Moreover, this study depicts special characters of the customers such as personality and social identities as intervening elements. Also, they are fulfilled social status by reviewing internal and external status of self-concept; as well as they want to how appeared among their friends. Absolutely, they are acting in different ways because specific/special clothes can give them the values which are employed affective and cognitive system. However, their special traits such as consciousness of product, tendency to new fashion, engaging with product, and being conductor their categories are correlated directly to the level of their shopping. The analysis of Goldsmith (2002) presented that these variables are due to their attitudes and personalities, and demographics information cannot be enough to determine factors for understanding consumers. Hence, the researcher should be taken advantage from psychological factors in order to segment target markets.

Zajas and Brewster (1995) surveyed about interpersonal success factors of managers who have more capability. Also, they demonstrated that the managers are who believe to control their different situations of organization with awareness. In addition, they can make the best strategy for transforming unstable situation to safe or high secure. Hence, LOC, self-esteem, adaptability, career involvement, and identity resolution are the factors which intervene to making-decision. Therefore, self-marketing of managers is based on their abilities which are comparing to other individuals mutually. Whereas the people who have less score on interpersonal factors of success, believe to fate and chance in their pros and cons as intervening factors. Moreover, they cannot able to handle own situation to switching specified opportunities.

2.4 Psychographics and Effectiveness

Since culture, social position and the context of personalities form a consumer's behaviors, and one choice is really center of ideas. So behaviors and choices are core of values. Also, the consumers are controlled by making decision from their options, when they are exposure in front of the media which advertise their selections. Consequently, one can select among different options that are based on social categories and relevant occupations which lead to their consumption patterns.

As the consequence of the marketing literature the position of consumer at the society is formed on the base of his/her needs and wants, understanding of lifestyle and personality. Also, the people almost distinguish the others in the society by evaluating their financial power or their budget which is allocated to the consumption patterns or leisure patterns (Veblen, 1975). However, one aspect of this evaluating comes out from tourism activities that can be presented the consumption and leisure patterns of individuals. Further, tourism provides the mixed services that can affect the consumers' relationships with their friends and environments (Beardsworth and Keil, 1997). Generally, customers prefer aesthetic versus of duty while they have motivated to choice products or services from tourism industrial. In addition, these products or services are intangible for customers at the first stage of purchasing, but they can be involved the customers' right needs and wants through the customers' role at social positions (Morrison et al, 1999). Moreover, the destination products are simulated by structured media and permanent imagines which can support the consumers' imagines (Williams, 2000). Hence, hospitality services can communicate the consumers' perceptions with the reality of products and services, while consumers are going to achieve their goals.

2.5 Conclusion

Psychographic segmentation is one of the best strategies for marketing research. Also, it can determine especial information from the customers who are in the different situations. In this chapter, psychographic segmentation is introduced such aspects that are mentioned in the marketing literature. It is noticeable that the psychographic for analyzing needs to demographic information from the consumers. In addition, marketers should be selecting good planning for improving their business by considering the circumstances of consumer in consumption patterns. Moreover, the tailoring planning on the basis of psychographic variables can give powerful tools to marketers. The next chapter is more discussed about the psychographic features in the tourism marketing.

CHAPTER 3

PSYCHOGRAPHICS IN TOURISM MARKETING

Tourism is a process of interchanging between customers and destination products; the customer comes to arbitrary destination for economically surplus. Also, he/she mediate with desires through socio-economic needs and wants. In addition, tourist is considered as end point of this interchange, and then operators intervene to acquire the consumers' satisfaction by promoting right products and services to them. Moreover, tourism industrial attempt to provide Maslow's hierarchy needs that related to psychographic variables of consumers who can be offered intangibility services included symbolical aesthetics. One aspect of tourism industrial is being a non-commercial which can reveal social role and potential personally of consumers (Arnold et al., 1998). In general, products or services of tourism industrial are going to the consumers' lifestyles and their identities that are related to psychological factors for provision of their needs and wants. Furthermore, they are chosen approaches which can present feelings, social differences, conceptions and affiliations (Gillespie, 1999). Therefore, tourism industrial is noticed as a live business for communicating variety groups of society and differences, but it has a very specific conception. For instance, one is purchasing service or product as consumer's behavior which is symbolical concept of him/her perception from right destination (Dann, 1998).

3.1 Customer Satisfaction

Marketers would like to produce new brands in order to retain consumers. The values factors can count as pivotal center to help marketers to grasp more satisfaction consumers. Also, strategies of segmentation through the psychographics criteria would be the most efficacy approaches to create more satisfied and loyal consumers. In addition, the literature presented that the cost of attracting new customers would be several times of retaining loyal consumers. As a result, customer satisfaction is the center of marketing which can act as a hub in a process of marketing to survey psychographic variables or other subjective norms.

Most of the successful companies employ Customer Satisfaction Measurements (CSM) or Customer Relationship Management (CRM) for retaining consumers for loyalty of their brand through the customer satisfaction. In addition, they consider the principles from customer oriented rules that make their firms culture. Moreover, the firms attempt to grasp satisfaction of consumers on the target market by offering good quality of products or services. Although the definitions of satisfaction are propounded from scholars, a product/service is purchased and used from the evaluation utility results. Hence, the level of expectations is very important factor to compare of products or service. When the results adapt to the expectation, then confirmation from customers will be occurred. Otherwise, we have disconfirmation which it has two folds as unsatisfied and delighted customers. If the results of comparing performances are shown less than the expectation level, so the output is negative disconfirmation, as well as better performance than the expectation level is positive disconfirmation. Hence, confirmation and positive disconfirmation are led to consumer satisfaction (Oliver and Desarbo, 1988; Tse and Wilton, 1988). The level of satisfaction is due to perception, evaluation and psyche from utility of goods/services. The level of expectation and perception can be changed by influencing external factors. Since the perception, culture, budget and lifestyle are difference among the different nations, so the people have different level of satisfaction. The marketer or stakeholders should offer suitable products and service respect to the level of expectations of customers on psychographic segmentation model (WTO, 1985).

.

In addition, the marketplace which has law and order, high quality of services and goods, friendly relationships with consumers, and dependable services can attract more tourists because of its reliability (Wang et al., 2010). Cultural and economical status can affect making-decision process for going abroad. Also, the customer motivations are related to cultures and status such as expressing oneself, reliability of destination, hedonic of traveling and having positive glances of the destination. The tourists always compare some factors like the culture, security and the facilities of transportation through the destination, while they can give encourage feelings to choice the destination and make loyalty feelings to it.

Another aspect of marketing destination is leading to branding destination. The first step to branding a destination is identifying its portfolio of products, then they suggest to the specific segments. They often exploit from the nature, historical events and places, cultures, infrastructures and facilities. Although the ads can affect from branding destination, the most effective way is word-of-mouth (WOM) through the relatives and acquaintances. Also, a positive WOM is created by the customers who experienced memorable traveling with good mood and vision of the destination. Hence, the people who live at the destination are helping tourists to get positive impression over the destination and are involved to the services/products. In addition, the prides of people influence on attitude of customers towards their positive WOM (Wangenheiem and Bayon, 2004; Grace and O'cass, 2002).

The studying of Reisinger and Turner (1999) identified that the tourism marketing and variety of cultures are important features in order to produce good perception of tourists. Moreover, expectations of tourists and their level of satisfaction are influenced by their own cultures. In fact, culture is a set of things or behaviors that are common among the people. Some nations have obeyed from own culture; the essential of their culture can influence on their making-decision process for planning trips. As a result, if the people would like to experience another culture, then the motivation for getting a decision to away would be the existence of differences between two cultures.

3.2 Typology of Tourism

According to Aguas et al. (2000), each of tourism establishes seeks the information from the tourism products, competitors and markets. Also, they want to assess right positioning at the markets. Tourism destinations should be pursued from attracting the potential tourists of target markets. Also, segmenting tourism market is a process that can divided tourism market into subgroups which have common wants and traits, when the destination is determined. The marketing of tourism markets is followed that the destination suggests what products and the tourism organizations seek what targets. So the developing of tourism products depends on portfolio of markets. Hence, Forecasting of changing markets and competitors information are valuable to sustain tourism destinations. Therefore, market size, market share and promotion of competitors are intervening to compute from determined competitors (Aguas et al., 2000).

However, Fascinating tours have created based on travelers' characteristics which really are customer-oriented, so the segmentation of those is very important for marketers. Hence, the marketers for attracting more customers should consider their lifestyles and preferences for selecting destinations, besides the planning should be tailored as a good plan for them. The former researches showed us there are several levels of tourism activities which are determined by measuring tourists' preferences. The tourists cannot be considered just by measuring their behaviors such as participating at the tours, because they have different emotions and experiences (Trauer, 2006). Also, the people have variety attitudes towards tourists that are reflected different believes from their daily life. The selecting of tourism package is depending on kinds of customers' diet, the internal challenges and attitudes. On the other hand, the psychographic variables are very important to measure tourist satisfaction through the performance of service quality and other infrastructure of the tourism destination.

Moreover, the tourism marketer should concern to attracting more tourists based on their desires, because the different tourists have different aspects needs or wants. For example, out-shopping is one's motivation who wants to go away for shopping. Also, cultural views of shopping create preferences and decisions of Image foreign brand is a symbolic value and high position in morality of consumers (Hui et al., 2003). In addition, traveling for business is carried out precisely by people who go away for business. While, it needs to fulfill businessmen or businesswomen wants as experience trip. The tourism marketers should provide right planning for them, because they have taken advantages from high tech. So leisure industry should use new brands and strategies in order to entice customers to retain them (Erdly and Kesterson-Towns, 2003).

Another typology of tourism marketing is pertaining to sport activities. The sports event is an approach to attracting tourists who are interested in attending sports places for watching or fan of their teams on the matches. In addition, visiting acquaintances such as relatives or friends is another motivation to travel. Exploiting regional of destination for researching, rest or sport experiences can be experienced by some tourists who pursue to adventure memorial trips. The youngest people are following their education which affects their future. They consider going away and getting new life for their goals. That is valuable experience for each international student.

Sometimes happening events for individuals compel them to go another place like disasters, tsunami, earthquake, famine or economical circumstances. Journalists have to go away for getting news or information for their media as tourists that is known as dark tourist. The aim of dark tourist is acquiring reliability news from the regions; some events have happened there and threaten humanities.

Someone visits away for health problem which is called health tourism. Recreation and nightlife of destination can be considered by some tourists as part of lifestyle and personality. Rural tourism appropriates for students who want to experience rural life as well as for tourists who want to utilize from rural environments.

3.3 Tourism Marketing and Segmentation

The studying of Silva and Correia (2008) explained that motivations, travel companions, money and time are more influencing factors for making-decision process. In addition, they consider these factors as intrapersonality, interpersonality and structural factors. Intrapersonality is as a psychological behavior that is related to psychographic traits, while interpersonality refers to the interaction or communicational situations with others like family or friends as well as structural factors have pointed about eco-society situations. Further, they considered these factors as facilitators and constraints in the leisure travels.

The concept of Special Interest Tours (SIT) refers to design tours based on the tourists' interests or their wants, and the tourism companies expect to consider the different plans based on individuals' needs. Actually, the SIT is growth slowly to become as a stable strategic plan for tourism marketing. According to Yang (1993), the special interest tours are applied on the segmentation of tourism marketing for attracting tourists towards specific packages or unique tours such as fashion clothes, golf, climbing mountain, culinary Arts, and so on. Indeed, SIT is formed by tourists' experiences with their specific interests (Douglas et al., 2001). Preferring specific activities, destinations or emotional travel programs can be known as SIT. Each method from SIT can attract different tourists, so it can create new business at the tourism markets (Sheng et al, 2008). Hence, SIT should be conformed to tourists' interests and wants; it has focused and limited because of the tourists' interests. On the other hand, the SIT travels don't need brand hotels or luxury life. It is ordered as remote destinations which are very hard to access or specific festivals appropriate with specific interests. It should be adjusted special events and have professional guides (Li, 1998). SIT is tailored by the marketers for grasping more tourists (Sorensen, 1993). Since SIT has been involved to the variety of recreation programs, it is gradually increasing (Douglas et al., 2001). While SIT segments customers only based on demographic variables for survey their needs and wants, it's better to add psychological variables to get useful methods. These needs are rungs of a Ladder as following Model:

Figure 3.1 the Ladder of Traveling

Needs and Wants

Source: Huang and Hsu (2009)

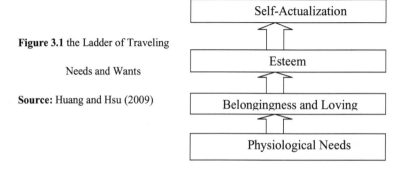

According to Maslow (1970), one is always to follow satisfying his/her needs and wants based on the hierarchical discipline, when one of levels is fulfilling then he/she goes on the next level. The next level is running as long as former level is fulfilled, so Maslow found out the fact of this order is depending on the level of fulfilling needs and wants on each level for going to the next level .

Pearce (1982) offered that a traveler has a motivation which is as an approach to follow or avoidance patterns. For example, a tourist who wants to go vacation on holiday, he/she will fulfill his/her physiological needs, belongingness and love, and self-actualization from hierarchical order. At first, he/she will seek the safety needs at the destination, and then pursue his/her physiological, love, esteem and self-actualization needs.

According to Huang and Hsu (2009), the hierarchical needs theory of Maslow is the most important in motivation researches. There is couple of theories in motivation researches as perception of motivation namely Travel Career Ladder (TCL) and Travel Career Patterns (TCP). The travelers' motivations are changed by experiencing of the travels; they are considered as relaxation, safety, relationship, self-esteem, development and fulfilling needs. So these characteristics of motivations are adjusted at the specific order. Many tourists are following ordered patterns which have proposed as travel motivations. Also, motivations and perceptions cause to ascend among their hierarchical needs when lower needs are satisfied. Changing motivation patterns are affected by tourists' healthy and their budget. In addition, the tourists who have more experience in trips eagerly pursued to fulfillment their high level needs. The main goal of TCL is ascending to high level needs of travelers with acquiring more experiences trips (Lee and Pearce, 2002). Further, TCP is followed by adjusting such types of TCL, but it is different from TCL (Lee and Pearce, 2002).

For example, Studying of Plog (1974) stated three situations for non-flyers American that are following:

1- Territory boundness: the people who have less tendency to trips in whole their life.
2- Generalize anxieties: the people who have strong fear from non-safety in their life.
3- A sense of powerless: the people who have less ability on events at their life.

These people are known as Psychocentrics which are clustered as dependable, near-dependable which they can accept more risk in their life. Oppositely, the people who accept more risk they put on Allocentrics group and they are self-assured. Also they clustered as near venture and venture. The distribution of these groups is normal and this model used broadly in many relevant books of tourism. This model is classifying people based on the amount of their venture (Huang and Hsu, 2009).

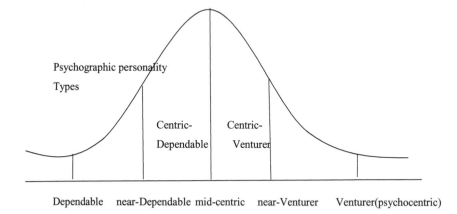

Figure 3.2 Allocenterism/ Psychocentrism Distribution

Source: Adapted from Plog (2001)

Programming of destinations are always seeking patterns which can predict to attract many type of tourists with different status, so these differences can be as factors for achieving the goals of the destinations. While the programmers of destinations want to develop hospitality industries, they should set up their services and disciplines. Initiating of introducing the destination is begun by a few numbers of venturers will visit from their destination. When they come back home and explain to their friends or relatives about their experiences , so some near-venturers will go there and after become satisfying and describe their experience to centric-venturer and centric-dependable friends, the destination confronts of increasing tourists over there. Dependable people are who follow others. Moreover, the marketers and hospitality industries can estimate and programming with confidence based on this model for investments. Population will increase at this time and then decrease gradually (Huang and Hsu, 2009).

Plog (2001) has pointed out an ideal psychographic status which can be used as middle of segmentation of near-venturer. The marketers can apply psychographic curve for understanding their customers for progress of hospitality industries and retain position of their destination. This model has disadvantages because it neither describes tourists' motivations nor predicts their behaviors. Mckercher (2005) has argued on validity of plog's model. For example, one would like to go winter vacation on allocentirc destination for skiing but his/her aim was psychocentric destination. Each tourist has different motivations at different situations; and is attracted toward destination which has unique relation respect to psychocentric/allocentric simultaneously. Plog's model can explain tourists' role and their lifestyle topology. It seems that model of Plog is considered for variety of tourist motivations in different lifestyle topologies (Huang and Hsu, 2009).

3.3.1 Psychographic Segmentation and Tourism

Voluntary simplicity is due from academic view of Gandhi life because of simplicity life. It is referred to internal attitudes and external experiences. For example, it presents internal aspects, faithful of personality, and loyalty of lifestyles. The customers have different lifestyles, so they have different interests and consumer behaviors. Ye (1985) has pointed out from the research group traveling, the people who have different lifestyles, so they have significant differences in selecting destinations.

Activities, interests and opinions as lifestyle factors are deeply affecting on tourism marketing for sustain tourism industries (Trauer, 2006). Also Voluntary Simplicity Lifestyle (VSL) is emphasized on simplicity, internal challenges and protecting ecological environment. The tourists who follow VSL are very autonomy and self-actualization (Sheng et al., 2008).

The Importance of tourism topics is due from tourists' lifestyles; the central of tourism issues from micro view can be affected by personal values. Both lifestyles and personal values are cause-effect relationships for environmental factors, supply and demands at the tourism marketing (Trauer, 2006). Hence, the personal values and lifestyles can use for segmentation as precise variables. Further, lifestyles conduct psychologically tourism products for attracting more people. Although some performances are not doing well or cannot succeed by brand names, they can be successful by lifestyles segmentation.

There are different aspects of tourism among the people from their attitudes and motivations that are shown believes respect to diversity daily works of them (Kuentzel, 2000). Also, the selecting of tourism companies and kind of tourism can be influenced by the diet, personality, expectations, and attitudes (Yuan et al., 2005; McKercher and Chan, 2005). The utmost importance of tourism issue would be kinds of activities, interests, and opinions which are reflected the expectations of people (Trauer, 2006). In general, people who follow simplicity, Voluntary Simplicity (VS) or Voluntary Simplicity Lifestyle (VSL), they protect their environment by consuming green products and defense from healthy of human being (Sheng et al., 2008).

3.4 Psychographic Variables in Tourism Literature

The previous investigations around tourism marketing have presented this market has formed different services and stages towards adapted tourists' lifestyles, socio-demographic, cultural values and their personalities. According to Gonzalez and Bello (2002), the hospitality industries are developing and the marketers pursue more attracting model because of personalization market. Hence, the demographic and socio-economic cannot be responsible for good segmentation. So, the applied variables would be as psychographic variables and demographics in tourism marketing researches. Those carried out into two dimensions which are led to general and specific researches. The former has been pointed out how to engage tourists with daily life without considering products or services roles, while the latter one has been surveyed rigorously tourists' psychographic dimensions.

Gonzalez and Bello (2002) stated that there is a correlation between lifestyle variables and tourist behaviors. Also, the findings of this study have presented positively correlations on the corresponding relationships which are estimated different lifestyle variables versus different tourist behaviors. Those variables could be influenced on segmentation of tourists.

However, Bigne et al. (2001) argued that difference and similarity between service quality and tourist satisfaction. In addition, they surveyed and examined those on the holiday experiences. Moreover, it is noticeable point that those concepts have differences and similarities meaning or definition in different objects or approaches. They believed that tourist's image from a destination is a key component of marketing which is related to service quality and tourist satisfaction. Also, high perception of service quality and satisfaction are the consequence of performances and comparing perceptions between ideal and real expectations of the destination which can lead to revisit intentions and recommend the destination. Moreover, satisfaction is considered as cognitive factor which is related to needs and wants generally, while service quality is considered as a desire of high perception from status of objects specifically. Further, tourist image has played the important role in hospitality marketing. It can influence in every construct of tourist behavior.

Buhalis (2000) explained that the destination can be considered as amalgam of service products which need to the best strategies for attracting more tourists. Also, they use the proper planning to coordinate different aspects or parts of the destination with local resources. The attributes of the destination can be interpreted by tourists subjectively based on their perceptions and previous experiences that is called tourist image. Tourism policy, facilities of destination and services are influencing this image from the tourists who are visiting the destination. Then attitude of tourists and marketers goals make provision of the destination. The tourism image obtains from communication these opportunities and profits of the destination. However, the tourism aims are very different through the travelers, as well as the issue of the segmentation for understanding tourist behaviors are being very sophisticated and complicated. Whole of stakeholders like tour agents, public sectors, and government are concerned to provide amenities for tourism sector. Moreover, stakeholders attempt to take advantage from the destination as a brand name and provide good image towards tourism loyalty. Hence, local resources are considered as core of marketing the destination and products/services. The provision of tourism sector emanates from tourism motivations, attitudes and values of selecting the destination that is related to the aim of visiting such as business like MICE (Meetings, Incentives, Conferences, and Exhibitions) or leisure traveling.

According Chen and Tasi (2007), service quality, satisfaction and tourist behaviors are associated to each other for attracting tourists. Also, tourist behaviors are run in three steps which are pre-, during-, and post visiting from the destination as tourism product. Each step is different from the other and has an evolution way to reach tourist intention. For instance, pre-visiting for choosing the destination, during-visiting for estimating trip quality and post-visiting for tourist intention. Also, Chen and Tasi (2007) stated that perceived value has been employed as moderating role between quality and satisfaction. In addition, the concept of perceived values is completely separate from quality and satisfaction concepts which are more effectiveness than two others for revisiting intentions. Hence, destination image can influence on perceived values and perceived values directly or indirectly affect on satisfaction and behavior intentions. Behavior intention of tourist refers to tourist judgment for revisiting intentions and recommend the destination by word-of-mouth , and perceived value refers to holistic estimating from received benefits versus given costs.

Figure 3.3 Satisfaction Model

Source: Chen and Tasi (2007)

The study of Chi and Qu (2008) has posited that attributes of the destination are related to satisfaction which is called attribute satisfaction. However, it is related to climate, nature of the destination and its culture, social situation and environment. Whereas overall satisfaction as a construct is related to experience of tourist from hospitality resources such as hotels, restaurant, recreation facilities and other amenities from the destination. Hence, destination image has positively associated to satisfaction; while satisfaction is influencing on destination loyalty. Also, destination image as a construct can affect on attribute satisfaction, next attribute satisfaction influences on overall satisfaction. Then overall satisfaction is leading to destination loyalty. While overall satisfaction is considered as a unique construct for presenting satisfaction, the factors of attribute satisfaction as a construct is pertaining to shopping, activities and events, lodging, accessibility, attractions, environment, dining. In addition, destination loyalties has two indicators such as revisit intention and recommend intention which are presented repurchasing service and WOM with high positive satisfaction.

3.5 Revisit Intention (RVI) and Recommend Intention (RCI)

Revisit intention of a specific destination through tourists is determined directly or indirectly on satisfaction which leads to loyalty of tourists. The tourist loyalty can be divided in three categories as behavioral loyalty, attitudinal loyalty or mixed them. Behavioral loyalty can be observed on repurchasing services, while attitudinal loyalty as the strength of effectiveness on the destination. The real loyal tourist who has these two dimensions of loyalty simultaneously. As tourism aspect, a loyal tourist is who would like to revisit or has revisit intention to the specific destination. Consequently, a positive awareness and image of a destination can introduce the destination as a brand. Because, awareness of destination is a concept which would be recognized as a specific destination among the others and image of destination is a total dimensions which are as images through the tourists. Therefore, the positive awareness and image of destination can be considered to affect the incentive stimulate for loyalty (Mechinda et al., 2010).

In addition, Kozak (2001) has pointed out the relationships among satisfaction levels of tourists with revisit destination and behavioral intentions. Also, the satisfaction levels are considered as focus discussing behavioral tourists' research and has presented as a model which is based on revisit of the destination, loyalty, and satisfaction. Moreover, assessing satisfaction variable is related to post hoc experience of the tourists from the destinations. However, gained information causes to distinguish the feedback of destination performances. So, the marketers and managers of the destination can recognize the best strategies in the future. Further, Kozak (2001) has explained that there is a difference between satisfaction and loyalty concepts which are adapted to intentions and expectations of tourists. Those lead to repurchase service. Therefore, positive perception and attitudes can be aimed in the tourism industry as a potential to create loyal tourists.

According to Alegre and Caldera (2009), satisfaction of tourists from the destination is the signal from different aspects of the destination towards tourists' perceptions. Moreover, the conceptual of satisfaction relates on motivation as internal push for visitors. However, revisit of the destination is presented as loyalty and low risk. Furthermore, the repeating to visit a destination and the satisfaction level of it demonstrate simultaneously endogenous variable can moderate between satisfaction and revisit intentions. Satisfaction can be affected by destination attributes such as geographical situation, hospitality, social life, price, quality, and motivation to revisit intentions.

Quintal and Polczynski (2010) asserted that satisfaction construct is influenced by perception of attractiveness, service quality, risk and value of the destination variables. In addition, the high degree satisfaction can lead to behavior intentions as RVI. They examined those characters on holiday destination for college students as tourists. Each of the factors of perception directly and indirectly is related to cognitive response, while satisfaction is considered as subjective response. Since some tourists prefer to visit familiar places, because of safety, time and budget. Revisit of the specific destination signs from the tourists' positive attitudes respect to what perceived from their previous experience at the destination. Generally, tourists would like to revisit because of good adventures and high benefit on pervious time which spend there. On the other hand, loyal tourists use word-of-mouth to their friends and relatives for offering the destination as holiday destination or other goals of tourism, so they can help stakeholders to reduce their cost in advertising of the tourism products as well as loyal tourists have interested for staying longer, shopping, dining and other attractiveness attributes from the destination. Hence, the loyal tourists can determine the specific and helpful strategy for tourism structures. Also, the tourists' attitudes from the first time visiting to revisiting the destination would be different. The tourism process for revisiting the destination is attitude, appraisal, emotional response, coping and behavioral intentions in orderly. The positive cognitive and affective responses from the tourists present their loyalty as attitudinal and behavioral as well as achieve their desires.

Quintal and Polczynski (2010) stated that the college students are more important as a revenue element for stakeholders at tourism sector. They have own lifestyle and personality in social categories which eagerly to experience new destination for understanding the people's lifestyle or utilizing on their education. Often, they are considered by age, social class, culture, education, their motivations and benefits. The destination attractive attributes are considered as facilities which different from tourist's home such as historical, recreation and entertainment places, nightlife, carnivals, events and services. In fact, tourist perception is related to their opinion and personal traits. Hence, perception of attractiveness, quality, risk and value are psychometric consistency, and satisfaction is an emotion of post hoc feature.

3.6 Conclusion

Consumer behaviors and psychology literature produce psychographic concept which can be presented on different categories of cultures, societies, traits and latent variables as to justify segmentations. However, correlation of psychographic and consumer behaviors leads to popular segmentations such as VALS, LOV, RVS, APT, and mean-ends chain technique (Harcar and Kaynak, 2008). This literature explained that segmentation history and its evolution to arrive global marketing concept. Also, it is described psychographic variables as latent variables which are affecting on affective and cognitive system. In addition, it has pointed to extend these concepts in tourism marketing. The noticeable point is to present relationships across these variables. Further, it is followed to segmentation approach in tourism marketing. Because of the tourists have different desires and circumstances. As a result, research marketing is following to discover and confirm the relationships among the constructs of markets and consumer behavior.

REFERENCES

Aguas, P., Costa, J., and Rita, P.(2000). A Tourist Market Portfolio for Portugal. International Journal of Contemporary Hospitality,12(7), 394-400.

Ahmad, N., Omar, A., and Ramayah, T. (2010). Consumer Lifestyle and Online Shopping Continuance Intention. Business Strategy Series, 11(4), 227-243.

Alegre, J. and Caldera, M. (2009). Analysing The Effect of Satisfaction and Previous Visits on Tourist Intentions to Return. European Journal of Marketing, 43(5/6), 670- 685.

Arnould, E., Price, L. , And Tierney, P. (1998). Communicative Staging of the Wilderness Servicescape. The service Industries Journal, 18(3), 91-115.

Babin, B.J. and Attaway, J. (2000). Atmospheric Affect as A Tool for Creating Value and Gaining Share of Customer. Journal of Business Research, 49 (2), 91-100.

Baker, D. and Crompton, J. (2000). Quality, Satisfaction and Behavioural Intentions. Annals of Tourism Research, 27(3), 785-804.

Balakrishnan, M. S. (2009). Commentary Strategic Branding of Destinations: A Framework. European Journal of Marketing, 43(5/6),611-629.

Beardsworth, A. and Keil, T.(1997). Sociology on the Menu, Routledge, London.

Beatty, S E. , Homer, P. M. and Kahle , L. R. (1998). Problems with VALs in International Marketing Research: An Example from an Application of the Empirical Mirror Technique. Advances in Consumer Research, 15, 375-380.

Bigne Alcaniz, E. B., Garcıa, I. S., and Blas, S. S. (2009). The Functional-Psychological Continuum in the Cognitive Image of a Destination: A Confirmatory Factor Analysis,Tourism Management ,30, 715-723.

Bigne, J. E., Sanchez, M. I. , and Sanchez, J. (2001). Tourism Image, Evaluation Variables and After Purchase Behaviour: Inter-Relationship. Tourism Management, 22, 607–616.

Boedeker, M. (1995). New-Type and Traditional Shoppers:A Comparison of Two Major Consumer Groups. International Journal of Retail & Distribution Management, 23(3), 17-26.

Bown J. T. (1998). Market Segmentation in Hospitality Research: No Longer a Sequential Process. International Journal of Contemporary Hospitality Management, 10(7), 289-296.

Brunsø, K., Scholderer, J. , and Grunert, K.G. (2004). Closing The Gap Between Values and Behavior – A Means-End Theory of Lifestyle. Journal of Business Research, 57(6), 665-70.

Buhalis, D. (2000). Marketing The Competitive Destination of The Future. Tourism Management, 21, 97-116.

Byon, K. ,and Zhang, J. (2010). Development of a Scale Measuring Destination Image. Marketing Intelligence & Planning, 28(4), 508-532.

Chen, C. ,and Tasi, D. (2007). How Destination Image and Evaluative Factors Affect Behavioral Intentions? Tourism Management, 28, 1115–1122.

Chi, C. G. and Qu, H. (2008). Examining The Structural Relationships of Destination Image, Tourist Satisfaction and Destination Loyalty: An Integrated Approach. Tourism Management, 29, 624–636.

Cowart, K.O., Fox, G.L. , and Wilson, A.E. (2008). A Structural Look at Consumer Innovativeness and Self-Congruence In New Product Purchases. Psychology& Marketing, 25(12), 1111-30.

Dann, G. (1998). The Pomo Promo of Tourism. Tourism , Culture & Communication, 1, 1-16.

Diaz-Martin, A.M., Iglesias, V., Vazquez, R. , and Ruiz, A. V.(2000). The Use of Quality Expectations to Segment a Service Market. Journal of Services Marketing,14(2),132-146.

Dibb, S., Stern, P. and Wensley, R. (2002). Marketing Knowledge and The Value of Segmentation. Marketing Intelligence and Planning, 20(2), 113-9.

Divine , R. L., And Lepisto, L.(2005). Analysis of the Healthy Lifestyle Consumer. Journal of Consumer marketing, 22(5), 275-283.

Dodd, C. A., Clarke, I., Baron, S. , And Houston, V. (2000). Looking the Part :
    Identity, Meaning and Culture in Clothing Purchasing- Theoretical
    Consideration. Journal of Fashion Marketing and Management,4(1), 41-48.

Douglas, M. and Isherwood, B.(1979). The World of Goods: Towards and
    Anthropology of Consumption. London: Allen Lane.

Douglas, N., Douglas, N., and Derret, R. (Eds) (2001). Special Interest Tourism.
    Melbourne: Wiley.

Engel, J., Blackwell, R. , and Kollat, D. (1978). Consumer Behavior : Hot.
    New York, NY : Rinehart and Wisnston.

Erdly, M. , & Kesterson-Townes, L. (2003). Experience Rules: A Scenario for the
    Hospitality and Leisure Industry Circa 2010 Envisions Transformation.
    Strategy & Leadership, 31(3), 12-18.

Future Brand (2006). Country Brand Index (2006). Available at: www.futurebrand.com
    /03chowcase/leadership/cbi/pdf/cbi_engo6.pdf (accessed 1 March 2007).

Gillespie, C. (1999). Current trends in Hotel Accommodation Design, in Verginis
    and Wood, R. C. (Eds), Accommodation Management: Perspectives for the
    International Hotel Industry, International Thomson Business Press, London.
    185-200.

Goldsmith, R. E. (2002). Some personality Traits of Frequent Clothing Buyers.
    Journal of Fashion Marketing and Management,6(3). 303-316.

Gonzalez, A. M. and Bello, L. (2002).The Construct " Lifestyle" in Market
    Segmentation the Behavior of Tourist Consumers. European Journal of
    Marketing, 36(1/2), 51-85.

Grace, D., and O'Cass, A. (2002). Brand associations: Looking Through The Eye of
    The Beholder. Qualitative Market Research: An International Journal, 5(2),
    96-111.
Grewal, R., Mehta, R., and Kardes, F. (2000). The Role of the Social-Identity
    Function of Attitudes in Consumer Innovativeness and Opinion Leadership.
    Journal of Economic Psychology, 21, 233-252.

Gunter, B., and Furnham, A. (1992), Consumer Profiles: An Introduction to
    Psychographics. London : Routledge.

Haley, R. (1968). Benefit Segmentation: A Decision Oriented Research Tool. Journal of Marketing, 30(3), 30-35.

Hallab, Z.A.A. (1999). An Exploratory Study of The Relationship Between Healthy-Living and Travel Behavior. Unpublished Dissertation. Virginia Polytechnic Institute and State University. Blacksburg, VA.

Hankinson, G. (2004).The Brand Images of a Tourism Destination: A Study of The Saliency of Organic Images. Journal of Product & Brand Management, 13(1), 6-14.

Hankinson, G. (2005). Destination Brand Image: A Business Tourism Perspective. Journal of Services Marketing, 19(1), 24-33.

Harcar, T. a. and Kaynak, E. (2008). Life-style Orientation of Rural US and Canadian Consumers :Are Regio-Centric Standardized Marketing Strategies Feasible?". Asia Pacific Journal of Marketing and Logistics, 20 (4), 433-454.

Hawkins, D.I., Best, R.J. and Coney, K.A. (2001), Consumer Behavior: Building Marketing Strategy.(8th ed.) New York, NY: McGraw-Hill.

Howard, J. A., and Sheth, J. (1969). The Theory of Buyer Behavior . New York, NY : John Wiley & Sons.

Hsu, C., Shih, M., Huang, B., Lin, B., and Lin,C. (2009). Predicting Tourism Loyalty Using an Integrated Bayesian Network Mechanism. Expert Systems with Applications ,36, 11760–11763.

Hsu, J.L., and Chang, K.-M. (2008). Purchase Clothing and Its Linkage to Family Communication and Lifestyle Among Young Adults. Journal of Fashion Marketing and Management, 12(2), 147-163.

Huang, S. And Hsu, C. (2009). Travel Motivation: Linking Theory to Practice. International Journal of Culture, Tourism, and Hospitality Research, 3(4), 287-295.

Hui, T. K., & Wan, D. T. W. (2003). Singapore's image as a tourist destination. International Journal of Tourism Research, 5, 305–313.

Hur, W., Kim, H. , and Park, J. (2010). Food- and Situation-Specific Lifestyle Segmentation of Kitchen Appliance Market. British Food Journal, 112(3), 294-305.

Hyllegard, K., Eckman, M., Descals, A. M. , and Borja, M. A. (2005). Spanish
    Consumers' Perceptions of U.S. Apparal Specialty Retilers' Products
    And Services. Jouranl of Consumer Behavior, 4(5), 345- 362.

IATA (2007). Passenger Numbers to Reach 2.75 Billion By 2011. Available At:
    www.iata.org/ pressroom/pr/2007-24-10-01 (Accessed 3 January 2007).

Jones, D. G. B. ,and Keep, W. (2009). Exploratons and Insights Hollander's
    Doctoral Seminar in The History of Marketing Thought. Journal of
    Historical Research in Marketing, 1(1), 151-164.

Kahle, L. and Chiagouris, C. (1996). Values, Lifestyles and Psychographics.
    NJ : Erlbaum.Hillsdale.

Kim, H.S. (2005). Consumer Profiles of Apparel Product Involvement and
    Values. Journal of Fashion Marketing and Management, 9 (2), 207-20.

Kotler P (1977). From Sales Obsession to Marketing Effectiveness. Harvard
    Business Review, 55 (November-December), 67-75.

Kotler, P. (1997). Marketing Management: Analysis, Planning, and Control.
    London :Prentice-Hall International (UK) Limited.

Kozak, M. (2001). Repeaters' Behavior at Two Distinct Destinations.
    Annals of Tourism Research, 28(3), 784–807.

Kropp, F. , Lavack, A. M. and Silvera, D. H. (2005). Values and Collective Self-Esteem
    As Predictors of Consumer Susceptibility to Interpersonal Influence
    among University Students. International Marketing Review, 22(1), 7-33.

Kucukemiroglu, O., Harcar, T. and Spillan, J.E. (2006).Market segmentation by
    Exploring Buyer Lifestyle Dimensions and Ethnocentrism Among Vietnamese
    Consumers: An Empirical Study. Journal of Asia-Pacific Business, 7 (4), 55-76.

Lee, H.-J. (2005).Influence of Lifestyle on Housing Preferences of Multifamily
    Housing Residents. Unpublished Dissertation, Virginia Polytechnic Institute
    and State University. Blacksburg, VA.

Lee, T. H. (2009). A Structural Model to Examine How Destination Image ,
    Attitude, and Motivation Affect the Future Behavior of Touist. Leisur
    Science, 31, 215-236.

Lee, U. and Pearce, P. (2002). Travel Motivation and Travel Career Patterns.
    Proceedings of 1st Asia Pacific Forum for Graduate Students Research in
    Tourism,17-35.

Li, X. (1998), New Thinking about Tourist, Yang-Chih Book Co. Ltd, Taipei.

Lin, C. (2002). Segmentation Customer Brand Preference: Demographic or Psychographic. Journal of Product & Brand Management, 11(4), 249-268.

Maslow, A. (1970), Motivation and Personality.(2nd ed.) New York, NY: Harper & Row.   .

McDonald, M. , and Dunbar, I. (2004), Market Segmentation: How To Do It. How To Profit From It. Butterworth-Heinemann, Oxford: Elsevier.

McKercher, B. , and Chan, A. (2005). How Special is Special Interest Tourism? Journal of Travel Research, 44(1), 21-31.

Mechinda, P., Seriat, S., Popaijit, N., Lertwannawit, A., and Anuwichanont, J. (2010). The Relative Impact of Competitveness Factors and Destinatin Equity on Tourist's Loyalty in Koh Chong, Thailand. The International Business & Econmics Research Journal, 9(10), 99-115.

Michman, R.D., Mazze, E.M. , and Greco, A.J. (2003). Lifestyle Marketing: Reaching the new American Consumer. Westport, CT :Praeger.

Michon, R., Chebat, J-C. and Turley, L.W. (2005). Mall Atmospherics: The Interaction Effects of The Mall Environment on Shopping Behaviour. Journal of Business Research, 58, 576-83.

Michon, R., Yu, H. And Smith, D.(2008). The Influence of Mall Environment on Female Fashion Shopper's Value and Behaviour. Journal of Fashion Marketing and Management, 12(4), 456-468.

Mitchel, V-W. (1995). Using Astrology in Market Segmentation. Management Decision, 33(1), 48-57.

Morrison, A. , Rimington, M., and Williams, C. (1999). Entrepreneurship in the Hospitality Tourism and Leisure Industries. Oxford: Butterworth-Heinemann.

Ng, I. C. L. (2005).Viewpoint: Does Direct Marketing Need to Have a Direction? Marketing Intelligence & Planning,23 (7),628-635.

Oliver, R. L. (1997). Satisfaction: A Behavioral Perspective on the Consumer. New York: McGraw Hill.

Oliver, R.L., and DeSarbo, W.S. (1988).Response Determinants in Satisfaction Judgments. Journal of Consumers Research,14, 495-507.

Olsen, S.O., Prebensen, N. ,and Larsen, T. A.(2009). Including Ambivalence as a Basis for Benefit Segmentation: A Study of Convenience Food in Norway. European Journal of Marketing, 34(5/6), 782-783.

Orth, U. R., McDaniel , M., Shellhammer, T., and Lopetcharat (2004). Promoting Brand Benefits: the Role of Consumer Psychographics and Lifestyle. Journal of Consumer Marketing, 21(2), 97-108.

Pearce, P. L. (1991). Fundamentals of Tourist Motivation. In Pearce, D.G and / Sutter , R.W (EDs) Tourism Research. Critiques and Challenge. London: Routlede.

Pearce, P.L. (1982), The Social Psychology of Tourist Behaviour. Oxford: Pergamon.

Pizam, A. and Ellis, T, (1999). Customer Satisfaction and its Measurement in Hospitality Enterprises. International Journal of Contemporary Hospitality Management,11(7), 326-339.

Plog, S.C. (1974).Why Destination Areas Rise and Fall in Popularity. Cornell Hotel and Restaurant Administration Quarterly, 14(4), 55-8.

Plog, S.C. (2001). Why Destination Areas Rise and Fall in Popularity: An Update of A Cornell Quarterly Classic. Cornell Hotel and Restaurant Administration Quarterly, 42(3), 13-24.
Plummer, J.T. (1974). The Concept and Application of Lifestyle Segmentation. Journal of Marketing, 38(1), 33-7.

Quinn, L., Hines, T. , And Bennison, D.(2007). Making Sense of Market Segmentation : A Fashion Retailing Case. European Journal of Marketing, 41 (5/6), 439- 465.

Quintal, V., and Polczynski, A. (2010). Factors Influencing Tourists' Revisit Intentions. Asia Pacific Journal of Marketing, 22(4), 554-578.

Raaij, W. F., and Verhallen, T. (1994). Domain specific Market Segmentation . European Journal of Marketing, 28 (10), 49-66.

Reed, A. (2002). Social Identity as a Useful Perspective for Self-Concept-Based Consumer Research. Psychology and Marketing, 19(3), 235-266.

Reisinger, Y. and Turner, L.(1999). A Cultural Analysis of Japanese Tourists: Challenges for Tourism Markets. European Journal of Marketing, 33(11/12), 1203-1227.

Rokeach, M. (1979). Understanding Human Values: Individual and Societal. New York, NY: Free Press.

Rokeach, M.J.(1973). The Nature of Human Values. New York,NY: the Free Press.

Roy, S.,and Goswami, P. (2007). Structural Equation Modeling of Value-Psychographic Trait-Clothing Purchase Behavior: A Study on The Urban College-Goers of India. Young Consumers ,8 (4),269-277.

Schiffman , L. G., And Kanuk, L. L. (2000). Consumer Behavior.(7th ed.) NJ :Prentice-Hall, Upper Saddle River.

Shavitt, S. (1989). Products, Personalities and Situations in Attitude Functions: Implications for Consumer Behavior . advances in Consumer Research, 16, 300-305.

Sheng, c., Shen, M. and Chen, M. (2008). Special Interest Tour Preferences and Voluntary Simplicity Lifestyle. International Journal of Culture, Tourism and Hospitality Research, 2(4),389-409.

Sorensen, L. (1993). The Special- Interest Travel Market. The General Hotel & Restaurant Administration Quarterly, 25(4), 24-30.

Stoel, L., Wickliffe, V. , and Lee, K.H. (2004). Attributes Beliefs and Spending as Antecedents to Shopping Value. Journal of Business Research, 57,1067-73.

Tam, J., and Tai, S. (1998).The Psychographic Segmentation of The Female Market in Greater China. International Marketing Review, 15(1), 61-77.

Tao, S.-P. (2006). A Cross-Cultural Comparison of Lifestyle Between Taiwanese and US consumers. Intercultural Communication Studies, XV(1), 43-57.

Taylor, S. A., and Baker ,T. L. (1994). An Assessment of the Relationship Between Service Quality and Customer Satisfaction in the Formation of Consumers' Purchase Intentions. Journal of Retailing, 70, 163-178.

Tse, D. K., and Wilton, P. C. (1988). Model of Consumer Satisfaction Formation: An Extension. Journal of Marketing Research, 25(2), 204-212.

Twedt, D. (1964). How Important to Marketing Strategy is The Heavy User?. Journal of Marketing, 28(1), 71-2.

Veblen,T. (1975[1899]). The Theory of the Leisure Class. New York. NY: Augustus, M. Kelly.
.

Villani, K., and Wind, Y. (1975). On The Usage of 'Modified' Personality Trait Measures in Consumer Research. Journal of Consumer Research, 2(December), 223-8.

Vyncke, P. (2002). Lifestyle Segmentation: From Attitudes, Interests and Opinions, to Values, Aesthetic Styles, Life Visions and Media Preferences. European Journal of Communication, 17(4), 445-63.

Wang, Y. J., Doss, S. K., Guo, C. , and Li, W (2010). An Investigation of Chinese Consumer's Out shopping Motives from a Culture Perspective: Implication for Retail and Distribution. International Journal of Retail and Distribution Management, 38(6), 423-442.

Wangenheim, F.V., and Bayo´n, T. (2004). The Effect of Word of Mouth on Services Switching: Measurement and Moderating Variables. European Journal of Marketing, 38(9/10), 1173-85.

Wedel, M. , and Kamakura, W.A. (1998). Market Segmentation: Conceptual and Methodological Foundations. London: Kluwer Academic Publishers.

Wells, W.D. (1975).Psychographics: A Critical Review. Journal of Marketing Research, 12, 196-213.

Wells,W.D., and Tigert, D.J. (1971). Activities, Interests and Opinions. Journal of Advertising Research, 11(4), 27-35.

Williams, A. (2000). Consuming Hospitality : Learning from Post-Modernism. In Lashley, C. And Morrison, A. (Eds). In Search Hospitality : Theoretical Perspectives and Debates.217-232 . Oxford: Butterworth-Heinemann.

Winters, L. C. (1992). International Psychographics. Marketing Research. Chicago. 4(3), 48-49.

Wolburg, J.M. and Pokrywczynski, J. (2001). A Psychographic Analysis of Generation y College sStudent. Journal of Advertising Research, 41(5), 33-50.

WTO (1985). Identification and Evaluation of those Components of Tourism Services which Have a Bearing on Tourist Satisfaction and which can be Regulated, and State Measures to Ensure Adequate Quality of Tourism Services. Madrid: World Tourism Organization.

WTTC (2007). World Travel and Tourism: Progress and Priorities 2007/2008. Available at: www. wttc.org/ (accessed 1 August 2007).

Yang, L.X. (1993). An Analysis of R.O.C. Nationals Tourism Consumer Behavior – The Case of The Residents of Taipei. Unpublished Master's Thesis. Department of Business Administration. National Sun Yat-Sen University: Kaohsiung.

Ye, Z.M. (1985). Analysis of Overseas Travelers' Psychological Segmentation and Their Preferences. Unpublished Master's Thesis. Department of Business Administration, National Cheng Chi University:Taipei.

Yeoh,P.L.(2005). A Conceptual Framework of Antecedents of Information Search in Exporting Importance of Ability and Motivation. International Marketing

Yuan, J., Cai, L.A., Morrison, A.M., and Linton, S. (2005). An Analysis of Wine Festival Attendees' Motivations: A Synergy of Wine, Travel and Special Events? Journal of Vacation Marketing, 11(1). 41-58.

Zajas, J., and Brewster, E. (1995). Beyond goal setting: key interpersonal success factors marketing executives today. Executive Development,8(3), 14-17.

MoreBooks!
publishing

yes

i **want** morebooks!

Buy your books fast and straightforward online - at one of world's fastest growing online book stores! Free-of-charge shipping and environmentally sound due to Print-on-Demand technologies.

Buy your books online at

www.get-morebooks.com

Kaufen Sie Ihre Bücher schnell und unkompliziert online – auf einer der am schnellsten wachsenden Buchhandelsplattformen weltweit! Versandkostenfrei und dank Print-On-Demand umwelt- und ressourcenschonend produziert.

Bücher schneller online kaufen

www.morebooks.de

VDM Verlagsservicegesellschaft mbH
Dudweiler Landstr. 99   Telefon: +49 681 3720 174   info@vdm-vsg.de
D - 66123 Saarbrücken   Telefax: +49 681 3720 1749   www.vdm-vsg.de

3955400R00048

Printed in Great Britain
by Amazon.co.uk, Ltd.,
Marston Gate.